JOY

JOY

The Happiness
That Comes from Within

OSHO

St. Martin's Griffin ❧ New York

www.stmartins.com

All books in the Insights for a New Way of Living series are created from
selected excerpts from the archive of original works by the author.

Cover art by Osho

Library of Congress Cataloging-in-Publication Data

Osho, 1931–1990.
    Joy / Osho.— 1st St. Martin's Griffin ed.
        p. cm. — (Insights for a new way of living)
    ISBN 0-312-32074-4
    1. Joy—Religious aspects. I. Title. II. Series: Osho, 1931–1990. Insights for a new way
of living.
    BP605.R34J69 2004
    299'.93—dc22

                                                                          2003019133

10   9   8   7   6   5   4

Contents

Contents

Foreword

Let me first tell you a small anecdote:

> *"My doctor insisted that I come to see you," the patient told the psychiatrist. "Goodness knows why—I am happily married, secure in my job, lots of friends, no worries . . ."*
>
> *"Hmmm," said the psychiatrist, reaching for his notebook, "and how long have you been like this?"*

Happiness is unbelievable. It seems that man cannot be happy. If you talk about your depression, sadness, misery, everybody believes it; it seems natural. If you talk about your happiness nobody believes you—it seems unnatural.

Sigmund Freud, after forty years of research into the human mind—working with thousands of people, observing thousands of disturbed minds—came to the conclusion that happiness is a fiction: Man cannot be happy. At the most, we can make things a little more comfortable, that's all. At the most we can reduce unhappiness a little, that's all, but happy? Man cannot be.

This sounds very pessimistic . . . but if you look at humanity, it seems to be exactly the case; it seems to be a fact. Only human beings are unhappy. Something deep down has gone wrong.

I say this to you on my own authority: Human beings *can* be happy, more happy than the birds, more happy than the trees, more happy than the stars—because human beings have something that no tree, no bird, no star, has. They have consciousness.

But when you have consciousness, two alternatives are possible: Either you can become happy or you can become unhappy. Then it is your choice. Trees are simply happy because they cannot be unhappy. Their happiness is not their freedom; they *have* to be happy. They don't know how to be unhappy; there is no alternative for them. The birds chirping in the trees are happy not because they have chosen to be happy—they are simply happy because they don't know any other way to be. Their happiness is unconscious; it is simply natural.

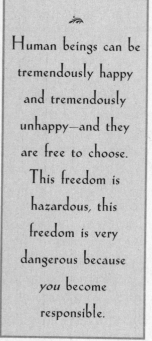

Human beings can be tremendously happy and tremendously unhappy—and they are free to choose. This freedom is hazardous, this freedom is very dangerous because *you* become responsible.

Human beings can be tremendously happy and tremendously unhappy—and they are free to choose. This freedom is hazardous; this freedom is very dangerous because *you* become responsible. And something has happened with this freedom, something has gone wrong. Man is somehow standing on his head.

People are seeking meditation. Meditation is needed only because you have not chosen to be happy. If you have chosen to be happy there is no need for any meditation. Meditation is medicinal: If you are ill then the medicine is needed. Once you have started choosing happiness, once you have decided that you will be happy, then no meditation is needed. Then meditation starts happening of its own accord.

There are so many religions because so many people are

unhappy. A happy person needs no religion; a happy person needs no temple, no church—because for a happy person the whole universe is a temple, the whole of existence is a church. The happy person does not pursue religious activity because his whole life is religious. Whatever you do with happiness is a prayer—your work becomes worship; your very breathing has an intense splendor to it, a grace.

Happiness happens when you fit with your life, when you fit so harmoniously that whatsoever you are doing is your joy. Then suddenly you will come to know that meditation follows you. If you love the work that you are doing, if you love the way you are living, then you are meditative. Then nothing distracts you. When things distract you, that simply shows that you are not really interested in those things.

> A happy person needs no religion, a happy person needs no temple, no church—because for a happy person the whole universe is a temple, the whole existence is a church.

The teacher goes on telling small children, "Pay attention to me! Be attentive!" They *are* attentive, but they are attentive to something else. A bird is singing with all its heart outside the school building—and the child is attentive to the bird. Nobody can say he is not attentive, nobody can say he is not meditative, nobody can say he is not in deep concentration—he is! In fact, he has completely forgotten the teacher and the arithmetic that the teacher is doing on the board. The child is completely oblivious to all that, he is utterly possessed by the bird and its song. But the teacher says, "Be attentive! What are you doing? Don't be distracted!"

In fact, the teacher is distracting the child! The child *is* attentive— it is happening naturally. Listening to the bird, he is happy. The teacher is distracting him, the teacher says, "You are not being attentive"—the teacher is simply lying! The child *was* attentive. The bird was more attractive to him, so what can he do? The teacher was not so attractive, the arithmetic had no appeal.

We are not put here on earth to be mathematicians. There are a few children who will not be interested in the bird; the song of the bird may go on getting louder and louder and they will be attentive to the blackboard. Then arithmetic is for them. Then they have a meditation, a natural meditative state, when it comes to mathematics.

We have been distracted into unnatural preoccupations: money, prestige, power. Listening to the birds is not going to give you money. Listening to the birds is not going to give you power, prestige. Watching a butterfly is not going to help you economically, politically, socially. These things are not profitable—but these things make you happy.

A real human being takes the courage to move with things that make him happy. If he remains poor, he remains poor; he has no complaint about it, he has no grudge. He says: "I have chosen my way—I have chosen the birds and the butterflies and the flowers. I cannot be rich, that's okay! I am rich because I am happy." But human beings have gone topsy-turvy.

I was reading:

Old Ted had been sitting on the edge of the river for some hours without getting a bite. The combination of several bottles of beer and a hot sun caused him to nod off, and he was completely unprepared when a lively fish got himself hooked, tugged at his line and woke him up. He was caught completely off balance and, before he could recover, found himself in the river.

A small boy had been watching the proceedings with interest.

As the man struggled to get out of the water, he turned to his father and asked, "Dad, is that man catching a fish or is that fish catching a man?"

Man has gone completely topsy-turvy. The fish is catching you and dragging you; you are not catching the fish. Wherever you see money, you are no longer yourself. Wherever you see power, prestige, you are no longer yourself. Wherever you see respectability, you are no longer yourself. Immediately you forget everything—you forget the intrinsic values of your life, your happiness, your joy, your delight. You always choose something from the outside, and you bargain for it with something from the inside. You gain the without and you lose the within.

But what are you going to do? Even if you get the whole world at your feet and you have lost yourself, even if you have conquered all the riches of the world and you have lost your own inner treasure, what are you going to do with your riches? This is the misery.

> Even if you get the whole world at your feet and you have lost yourself, even if you have conquered all the riches of the world and you have lost your own inner treasure, what are you going to do with your riches?

If you can learn one thing, that one thing is to be alert, aware, about your own inner motives, about your own inner destiny. Never lose sight of it, otherwise you will be unhappy. And when you are unhappy, people will say: "Meditate and you will become happy." They say: "Pray and you will become happy; go to the temple, be religious, be a Christian or a Hindu and you will be happy." This is all nonsense. Be happy, and meditation will follow. Be happy, and religiousness will follow. Happiness is the basic condition.

But people become religious only when they are unhappy—then their religion is pseudo. Try to understand why you are unhappy. Many people come to me and they say they are unhappy and they want me to give them some meditation. I say, first, the basic thing is to understand why you are unhappy. If you don't remove those basic causes of your unhappiness, you can meditate but that is not going to help very much—because the basic causes will remain there.

> You don't have anything to put at the stake, only your unhappiness, your misery. But people cling even to that.

Someone may have been a beautiful dancer and she is sitting in an office, piling up files. There is no possibility for dance. Someone may have enjoyed dancing under the stars, but he is simply accumulating a bank balance. And these people say they are unhappy: "Give me some meditation to do." I can give it—but what is that meditation going to achieve? What is it supposed to do? They will remain the same persons, accumulating money, competitive in the marketplace. The meditation may help in making them a little more relaxed, so that they can do this nonsense even better.

You can repeat a mantra, you can do a certain meditation; it can help you a little bit here and there—but it can only help you to remain whatever you are. It is not a transformation.

Hence, my approach is for those who are really daring, for the daredevils who are ready to change their very pattern of life, who are ready to stake everything—because in fact you don't have anything to stake; only your unhappiness, your misery. But people cling even to that.

I have heard:

In a remote training camp, a squad of rookies had just
returned to their billet after a day's march under the broil-
ing sun.

"What a life!" said one new soldier. "Miles from anywhere, a sergeant who thinks he's Attila the Hun, no
women, no booze, no leave—and on top of all that, my
boots are two sizes too small."

"You don't want to put up with that, chum," said his
neighbor. "Why don't you put in for another pair?"

"Not likely," came the reply. "Taking 'em off is the
only pleasure I've got!"

What else do you have to stake? Just your misery. The only
pleasure you have is talking about it. Look at people talking about
their misery, how happy they become! They pay for it; they go to
psychoanalysts to talk about their misery—they pay for it! Somebody listens attentively, and they are very happy.

People talk about their misery again and again and again. They
even exaggerate, they embellish it, they make it look bigger. They
make it look bigger than life-size. Why? You have nothing but your
misery at stake, but people cling to the known, to the familiar. The
misery is all they have known; that is their life. Nothing to lose, but
so afraid to lose it.

As I see it, happiness comes first, joy comes first. A celebrating
attitude comes first. A life-affirming philosophy comes first. Enjoy!
If you cannot enjoy your work, change. Don't wait! Because all the
time that you are waiting you are waiting for Godot and Godot is
never going to come. One simply waits and wastes one's life. For
whom, for what are you waiting?

If you see the point, that you are miserable in a certain pattern
of life; then all the old traditions say *you* are wrong—I would like

to say the *pattern* is wrong. Try to understand the difference of emphasis. You are not wrong, just your pattern; the way you have learned to live is wrong. The motivations that you have learned and accepted as yours are not yours—they don't fulfill your destiny. They go against your grain, they go against your element.

Remember it: Nobody else can decide for you. All their commandments, all their orders, all their moralities, serve to cripple you. You have to decide for yourself, you have to take your life in your own hands. Otherwise, life goes on knocking at your door and you are never there—you are always somewhere else.

If you were going to be a dancer, life comes from that door because life thinks you must be a dancer by now. It knocks on that door, but you are not there—you are a banker. How is life expected to know that you would become a banker? Life comes to you the way your nature wanted you to be; it knows only that address—but you are never found there, you are somewhere else, hiding behind somebody else's mask, in somebody else's garb, under somebody else's name. Existence goes on searching for you. It knows your name, but you have forgotten that name. It knows your address, but you have never lived at that address. You allowed the world to distract you.

> "I dreamt I was a kid last night," Joe was telling Al, "and I had a free pass to all the rides at Disneyland. Boy, what a time I had! I didn't have to choose which rides to go on— I rode them all."
>
> "That's interesting," remarked his friend. "I had a vivid dream last night too. I dreamt a beautiful blonde knocked on my door and overwhelmed me with her desire. Then just as we were getting started, another visitor, a gorgeous well-stacked brunette, came in and wanted me too!"
>
> "Wow," interrupted Joe. "Boy, would I have loved to be there! Why didn't you call me?"

"I did," responded Al. "And your mother told me you were at Disneyland."

Your destiny can find you in only one way, and that is your inner flowering, as existence wanted you to be. Unless you find your spontaneity, unless you find your element, you cannot be happy. And if you cannot be happy, you cannot be meditative.

Why did this idea arise in people's minds that meditation brings happiness? In fact, wherever they found a happy person they always found a meditative mind—the two things became associated. Whenever they found a beautiful, meditative milieu surrounding a person, they always found that person was tremendously happy—vibrant with bliss, radiant. They became associated. People thought happiness comes when you are meditative.

It is just the other way around: Meditation comes when you are happy. But to be happy is difficult and to learn meditation is easy. To be happy means a drastic change in your way of life—an abrupt change, because there is no time to lose. A sudden change, a discontinuity, a discontinuity with the past. A sudden clash of thunder and you die to the old and you start afresh from ABC. You again start your life as you would have done if there had been no pattern enforced by your parents, by your society, by the state; as you would have done, *must* have done, if there had been nobody to distract you. But you were distracted.

You have to drop all those patterns that have been forced on you, and you have to find your own inner flame.

WHAT IS HAPPINESS?

Happiness has nothing to do with success, happiness has nothing to do with ambition, happiness has nothing to do with money, power, prestige. Happiness has something to do with your consiousness, not with your character.

IT DEPENDS ON YOU

What is happiness? It depends on you, on your state of consciousness or unconsciousness, whether you are asleep or awake. There is one famous maxim of Murphy. He says there are two types of people: one who always divides humanity into two types, and the other, who doesn't divide humanity at all. I belong to the first type: Humanity can be divided into two types, the sleeping ones and the awakened ones—and, of course, a small group in between.

Happiness will depend on where you are in your consciousness. If you are asleep, then pleasure is happiness. Pleasure means sensation, trying to achieve something through the body that is not possible to achieve through the body—forcing the body to achieve something it is not capable of. People are trying, in every possible way, to achieve happiness through the body.

The body can give you only momentary pleasures, and each pleasure is balanced by pain in the same amount, to the same degree. Each pleasure is followed by its opposite because the body exists in the world of duality. Just as the day is followed by night and death is followed by life and life is followed by death; it is a vicious circle. Your pleasure will be followed by pain, your pain will be followed by pleasure. But you will never be at ease. When you are in a state of pleasure you will be afraid that you are going to lose it, and that fear will poison it. And when you are lost in pain, of course, you will be in suffering and you will make every possible effort to get out of it—only to fall back into it again.

Buddha calls this the wheel of birth and death. We go on moving with this wheel, clinging to the wheel . . . and the wheel moves on. Sometimes pleasure comes up and sometimes pain comes up, but we are crushed between these two rocks.

But the sleeping person knows nothing else. He knows only a few sensations of the body—food, sex; this is his world. He goes on moving between these two. These are the two ends of his body: food and sex. If he represses sex he becomes addicted to food; if he represses food he becomes addicted to sex. Energy goes on moving like a pendulum. And whatever you call pleasure is, at the most, just relief from a tense state.

Sexual energy gathers, accumulates; you become tense and heavy and you want to release it. To the man who is asleep, sexuality is nothing but a relief, like a good sneeze. It gives him nothing but a certain relief—a tension was there, now it is no longer there. But it will accumulate again. Food gives you only a little taste on the tongue; it is not much to live for. But many people are living only to eat; there are very few people who eat to live.

The story of Columbus is well known. It was a long trip. For three months they saw nothing but water. Then one day Columbus looked out at the horizon and saw trees. And if you think Columbus was happy to see trees, you should have seen his dog!

This is the world of pleasure. The dog can be forgiven, but you cannot be forgiven.

During their first date, the young man, looking for ways to have a good time, asked the young lady if she would like to go bowling. She replied that she did not care to go bowling. He then suggested a movie, but she answered that she did not care for them. While trying to think of something else he offered her a cigarette, which she declined. He then asked if she would like to dance and drink at the new disco. She again declined by saying she did not care for those things.

In desperation he asked her to come to his apartment for a night of lovemaking. To his surprise she happily agreed, kissed him passionately, and said, "You see, you don't need any of those other things to have a good time!"

What we call "happiness" depends on the person. To the sleeping person, pleasurable sensations are happiness. The sleeping person lives from one pleasure to another pleasure. He is just rushing from one sensation to another sensation. He lives for small thrills; his life is very superficial. It has no depth, it has no quality. He lives in the world of quantity.

Then there are people who are in between, who are neither asleep nor awake, who are just in a limbo, a little bit asleep, a little bit awake. You sometimes have that experience in the early morning— still sleepy, but you can't say you are asleep because you can hear the noise in the house, your partner preparing tea, the noise of the kettle or the children getting ready to go to school. You can hear these things, but still you are not awake. Vaguely, dimly, these noises reach you, as if there is a great distance between you and all that is happening around you. It feels as if it is still part of a dream. It is not part of a dream, but you are in a state of in-between.

The same happens when you start meditating. The nonmeditator sleeps, dreams; the meditator starts moving away from sleep toward awakening, is in a transitory state. Then happiness has a totally different meaning: It becomes more of a quality, less of a quantity; it is more psychological, less physiological. The meditator enjoys music more, enjoys poetry more, enjoys creating something. These people enjoy nature, its beauty. They enjoy silence, they enjoy what they had never enjoyed before, and this is far more lasting. Even if the music stops, something lingers on in you.

And it is not a relief. The difference between pleasure and this quality of happiness is that it is not a relief, it is an enrichment. You become more full, you start overflowing. While you listen to good music, something is triggered in your being, a harmony arises in you—you become musical. Or dancing, suddenly you forget your body; your body becomes weightless. The grip of gravity over you is lost. Suddenly you are in a different space: The ego is not so solid, the dancer melts and merges into the dance.

> Now is the only
> time and here
> is the only space.
> And then suddenly
> the whole sky
> drops into you.
> This is bliss.
> This is real happiness.

This is far higher, far deeper, than the pleasure you gain from food or sex. This has a depth. But this is also not the ultimate. The ultimate happens only when you are fully awake, when you are a buddha, when all sleep is gone and all dreaming is gone—when your whole being is full of light, when there is no darkness within you. All darkness has disappeared and with that darkness, the ego is gone. All tensions have disappeared, all anguish, all anxiety. You are in a state of total contentment. You live in the present; no past, no future anymore. You are utterly here now. This moment is all. Now is the only time and here is the only space. And then suddenly the whole sky drops into you. This is bliss. This is real happiness.

Seek bliss; it is your birthright. Don't remain lost in the jungle of pleasures; rise a little higher. Reach to happiness and then to bliss. Pleasure is animal, happiness is human, bliss is divine. Pleasure binds you, it is a bondage, it chains you. Happiness gives you a little more rope, a little bit of freedom, but only a little bit. Bliss is absolute freedom. You start moving upward; it gives you wings. You are no longer part of the gross earth; you become part of the sky. You become light, you become joy.

Pleasure is dependent on others. Happiness is not so dependent on others, but still it is separate from you. Bliss is not dependent, it is not separate either; it is your very being, it is your very nature.

FROM THE SURFACE TO THE CENTER

Gautam Buddha has said:
There is pleasure and there is bliss.
Forgo the first to possess the second.
Meditate over it as deeply as possible, because it contains one of the most fundamental truths. These four words will have to be understood, pondered over: the first is *pleasure*; the second, *happiness*; the third is *joy*; and the fourth is *bliss*.

Pleasure is physical, physiological. Pleasure is the most superficial thing in life; it is titillation. It can be sexual, it can be of other senses, it can become an obsession with food, but it is rooted in the body. The body is your periphery, your circumference; it is not your center. And to live on the circumference is to live at the mercy of all kinds of things that go on happening around you. The man who seeks pleasure remains at the mercy of accidents. It is like the waves in the ocean; they are at the mercy of the winds. When strong winds come, the waves are there; when the winds disappear, the waves disappear. They don't have an independent existence, they are dependent—and anything that is dependent on something outside of itself brings bondage.

Pleasure is dependent on the other. If you love a woman, if that is your pleasure, then that woman becomes your master. If you love a man—if that is your pleasure and you feel unhappy, in despair, sad, without him—then you have created bondage for yourself. You have created a prison, you are no longer in freedom. If you are a seeker after money and power, then you will be dependent on money and power. The man who goes on accumulating money, if it is his pleasure to have more and more money, will become more and more miserable—because the more he has, the more he wants, and the more he has, the more he is afraid to lose it.

It is a double-edged sword: wanting more is the first edge of the sword. The more you demand, the more you desire, the more you feel yourself lacking something—the more hollow, empty, you appear to yourself. And the other edge of the sword is that the more you have, the more you are afraid it can be taken away. It can be stolen. The bank can fail, the political situation in the country can change, the country can go communist . . . there are a thousand and one things upon which your money depends. Your money does not make you a master, it makes you a slave.

Pleasure is peripheral; hence it is bound to depend on outer circumstances. And it is only titillation. If food is pleasure, what actually is being enjoyed? Just the taste—for a moment, when the food passes across the taste buds on your tongue, you feel a sensation that you interpret as pleasure. It is your interpretation. Today it may look like pleasure and tomorrow it may not look like pleasure; if you go on eating the same food every day your taste buds will become unresponsive to it. Soon you will be fed up with it.

That's how people become fed up—one day you are running after a man or a woman and the next day you are trying to find an excuse to get rid of the same person. The same person—nothing has changed! What has happened meanwhile? You are bored with the other, because the whole pleasure was in exploring the new. Now the other is no longer new; you are acquainted with their territory. You are acquainted with the body of the other, the curves of the body, the feel of the body. Now the mind is hankering for something new.

The mind is always hankering for something new. That's how the mind keeps you always tethered somewhere in the future. It keeps you hoping, but it never delivers the goods—it cannot. It can only create new hopes, new desires.

The mind is always hankering for something new. That's how the mind keeps you always tethered somewhere in the future. It keeps you hoping, but it never delivers the goods.

Just as leaves grow on the trees, desires and hopes grow in the mind. You wanted a new house and now you have it—and where is the pleasure? Just for a moment it was there, when you achieved your goal. Once you have achieved your goal, your mind is no longer interested in it; it has already started spinning new webs of desire. It has already started thinking of other, bigger houses. And this is so about everything.

Pleasure keeps you in a neurotic state, restless, always in turmoil. So many desires, and every desire unquenchable, clamoring for attention. You remain a victim of a crowd of insane desires—insane because they are unfulfillable—and they go on dragging you in different directions. You become a contradiction. One desire takes you to the left, another toward the right, and simultaneously you go on nourishing both the desires. And then you feel a split, then you feel divided, you feel torn apart. Then you feel as if you are falling into pieces. Nobody else is responsible; it is the stupidity of desiring pleasure that creates this situation.

And it is a complex phenomenon. You are not the only one who is seeking pleasure; millions of people just like you are seeking the same pleasures. Hence there is great struggle, competition, violence, war. All have become enemies to each other because they are all seeking the same goal—and not all of them can have it. Hence the struggle has to be total, you have to risk all—and for nothing, because when you gain, you gain nothing. Your whole life is wasted in this struggle. A life that could have been a celebration becomes a long, drawn-out, unnecessary struggle.

When you are so wrapped up in seeking pleasure you cannot love, because the person who seeks pleasure uses the other as a means. And to use the other as a means is one of the most immoral acts possible, because each being is an end unto himself, you cannot use the other as a means. But in seeking pleasure you have to use the other as a means. You become cunning because it is such a struggle. If you are not cunning you will be deceived, and before others deceive you, you have to deceive them.

Machiavelli has advised pleasure seekers that the best way of defense is to attack. Never wait for the other to attack you; that may be too late. Before the other attacks you, you attack him! That is the best way of defense. And this is being followed, whether people know about Machiavelli or not.

This is something very strange:

> People don't know much about Machiavelli, but they follow him—as if Machiavelli is very close to their hearts. You need not read him, you are already following him.

People know about Christ, about Buddha, about Mohammed, about Krishna, and nobody follows them. People don't know much about Machiavelli, but they follow him—as if Machiavelli is very close to their hearts. You need not read him, you are already following him. Your whole society is based on Machiavellian principles; that's what the whole political game is all about. Before somebody snatches anything from you, snatch it from them; always be on guard. Naturally, if you are always on guard you will be tense, anxious, worried. Everyone is against you and you are against everybody else.

So pleasure is not and cannot be the goal of life.

The second word to be understood is happiness. Pleasure is physiological, happiness is psychological. Happiness is a little better, a little more refined, a little higher . . . but not very much different from pleasure. You can say that pleasure is a lower kind of happiness and happiness is a higher kind of pleasure— two sides of the same coin. Pleasure is a little primitive, animal; happiness is a little more cultured, a little more human—but it is the same game played in the world of the mind. You are not so concerned with physiological sensations, you are much more concerned with psychological sensations. But basically they are not different.

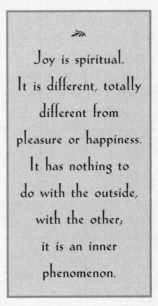

Joy is spiritual. It is different, totally different from pleasure or happiness. It has nothing to do with the outside, with the other, it is an inner phenomenon.

The third is joy—joy is spiritual. It is different, totally different from pleasure or happiness. It has nothing to do with the outside, with the other; it is an inner phenomenon. Joy is not dependent on circumstances; it is your own. It is not a titillation produced by things; it is a state of peace, of silence—a meditative state. It is spiritual.

But Buddha has not talked about joy either, because there is still one thing that goes beyond joy. He calls it bliss. Bliss is total. It is neither physiological nor psychological nor spiritual. It knows no division, it is indivisible. It is total in one sense and transcendental in another sense. Buddha uses only two words in this saying. The first is *pleasure*; it includes happiness. The second is *bliss*; it includes joy.

Bliss means you have reached to the very innermost core of your being. It belongs to the ultimate depth of your being where even the ego is no more, where only silence prevails; you have disappeared. In joy you exist a little bit, but in bliss you are not. The ego has dissolved; it is a state of nonbeing.

Buddha calls it "nirvana." Nirvana means you have ceased to be; you are just an infinite emptiness like the sky. And the moment you are that infinity, you become full of the stars, and a totally new life begins. You are reborn.

Pleasure is momentary, it belongs to time, it is "for the time being"; bliss is nontemporal, timeless. Pleasure begins and ends; bliss abides forever. Pleasure comes and goes; bliss never comes, never goes—it is already there in the innermost core of your being. Pleasure has to be snatched away from the other; you become either a beggar or a thief. Bliss makes you a master.

Bliss is not something that you invent but something that you discover. Bliss is your innermost nature. It has been there since the very beginning, you just have not looked at it. You have taken it for granted. You don't look inward.

This is the only misery of man: that he goes on looking outward, seeking and searching. And you cannot find it in the outside because it is not there.

One evening, Rabiya—she was a famous Sufi mystic—was searching for something on the street in front of her small hut. The sun was setting; slowly, slowly, darkness was descending. A few people gathered. They asked her, "What are you doing? What have you lost? What are you searching for?"

She said, "I have lost my needle."

The people said, "Now the sun is setting and it will be very difficult to find the needle, but we will help you. Where exactly has it fallen? Because the road is big and the needle is so small. If we know the exact place it will be easier to find it."

Rabiya said, "It is better not to ask me that question—because in fact it has not fallen on the road at all, it has fallen inside my house."

The people started laughing and they said, "We always thought that you were a little insane! If the needle has fallen inside the house, then why are you searching on the road?"

Rabiya said, "For a simple, logical reason: Inside the house there is no light and on the outside a little light is still there."

The people laughed and started dispersing. Rabiya called them back and said, "Listen! That's exactly what you are doing; I was just following your example. You go on seeking bliss in the outside world without asking the first and primary question: Where have you lost it? And I tell you, you have lost it inside. You are looking for it on the outside for the simple, logical reason that your senses open outward—there is a little more light. Your eyes look outward, your ears hear outward, your hands reach outward; that's the reason why you are searching outside. Otherwise, I tell you, you have not lost it there—and I tell you on my own authority. I have also searched on the outside for many, many lives, and the day I looked in I was surprised. There was no need to seek and search; it has always been within."

Bliss is your innermost core. Pleasure you have to beg from others; naturally you become dependent. Bliss makes you a master. Bliss is not something that happens; it is already the case.

Buddha says: *There is pleasure and there is bliss. Forgo the first to possess the second.* Stop looking on the outside. Look within, turn in.

Start seeking and searching in your own interiority, your own subjectivity. Bliss is not an object to be found anywhere else; it is your consciousness.

In the East we have always defined the ultimate truth as *Sat-Chit-Anand*. *Sat* means truth, *chit* means consciousness, *anand* means bliss. They are three faces of the same reality. This is the true trinity, not God the Father, the Son, Jesus Christ, and the Holy Ghost; that is not the true trinity. The true trinity is truth, consciousness, bliss. And they are not separate phenomena, but one energy expressed in three ways, one energy with three faces. Hence in the East we say God is *trimurti*—God has three faces. These are the real faces—not Brahma, Vishnu, and Mahesh, those are for children, for those who are spiritually, metaphysically immature. Brahma, Vishnu, and Mahesh; the Father, the Son, the Holy Ghost—those names are for beginners.

Truth, consciousness, bliss—these are the ultimate truths. First comes truth. As you enter, you become aware of your eternal reality—*sat*, truth. As you go deeper into your reality, into your truth, you become aware of consciousness, a tremendous consciousness. All is light, nothing is dark. All is awareness, nothing is unawareness. You are just a flame of consciousness, not even a shadow of unconsciousness anywhere. And when you enter still deeper, then the ultimate core is bliss—*anand*.

Buddha says: *Forgo everything that you have thought meaningful, significant, up to now.* Sacrifice everything for this ultimate because this is the only thing that will make you contented, that will make you fulfilled, that will bring spring to your being . . . and you will blossom into a thousand and one flowers.

Pleasure will keep you a driftwood. Pleasure will make you more and more cunning; it will not give you wisdom. It will make you more and more a slave; it will not give you the kingdom of your being. It will make you more and more calculating, it will make you more and more exploitative. It will make you more and more political, diplomatic. You will start using people as means; that's what people are doing.

The husband says to the wife, "I love you," but in reality he simply uses her. The wife says she loves the husband, but she is simply using him. The husband may be using her as a sexual object and the wife may be using him as financial security. Pleasure makes everybody cunning, deceptive. And to be cunning is to miss the bliss of being innocent, is to miss the bliss of being a child.

At Lockheed, a part was needed for a new airplane and an announcement was sent around the world to get the lowest bid. From Poland came a bid of three thousand dollars. England offered to build the part for six thousand. The asking price from Israel was nine thousand. Richardson, the engineer in charge of constructing the new plane, decided to visit each country to find out the reason behind the disparity of the bids.

In Poland, the manufacturer explained, "One thousand for the materials needed, one thousand for the labor, and one thousand for overhead and a tiny profit."

In England, Richardson inspected the part and found that it was almost as good as the Polish-made one. "Why are you asking six thousand?" inquired the engineer. "Two thousand for material," explained the Englishman, "two thousand for labor, and two thousand for expenses and a small profit."

In Israel, the Lockheed representative wandered through a back alley into a small shop and encountered an elderly man who had submitted the bid of nine thousand dollars. "Why are you asking that much?" he asked.

"Well," said the old Jew, "three thousand for you, three thousand for me, and three thousand for the schmuck in Poland!"

Money, power, prestige—they all make you cunning. Seek pleasure and you will lose your innocence, and to lose your innocence is to lose all. Jesus says: Be like a small child, only then can you enter into the Kingdom of God. And he is right. But the pleasure seeker cannot be as innocent as a child. He has to be very clever, very cunning, very political; only then can he succeed in the cutthroat competition that exists all around. Everybody is at everybody else's throat, you are not living among friends. The world cannot be friendly unless we drop this idea of competitiveness.

But from the very beginning we start corrupting every child with this poison of competitiveness. By the time he comes out of the university he will be completely poisoned. We have hypnotized him with the idea that he has to fight with others, that life is a survival of the fittest. Then life can never be a celebration.

If you are happy at the expense of another man's happiness . . . and that is how you can be happy, there is no other way. If you find a beautiful woman and somehow manage to possess her, you have snatched her away from others' hands. We try to make things look as beautiful as possible, but it is only on the surface. Now the others who have lost in the game will be angry, in a rage. They will wait for their opportunity to take revenge, and sooner or later that moment will come.

> Use whatever happens to be with you in the moment, but don't be possessive. Don't try to claim that it is yours. Nothing is yours, all belongs to existence.

Whatever you possess in this world you possess at somebody else's expense, at the cost of somebody else's pleasure. There is no other way. If you really want not to be inimical to anybody in the world, you have to drop the whole idea of possessiveness. Use whatever happens to be with you in the moment, but don't be possessive. Don't try to claim that it is yours. Nothing is yours, all belongs to existence.

EMPTY HANDS

We come with empty hands and we will go with empty hands, so what is the point of claiming so much in the meantime? But this is what we know, what the world tells us: possess, dominate, have more than others have. It may be money or it may be virtue; it does not matter in what kind of coins you deal—they may be worldly, they may be otherworldly. But be very clever, otherwise you will be exploited. Exploit and don't be exploited—that is the subtle message given to you with your mother's milk. And every school, college, university, is rooted in the idea of competition.

A real education will not teach you to compete; it will teach you to cooperate. It will not teach you to fight and come first. It will teach you to be creative, to be loving, to be blissful, without comparing yourself to others. It will not teach you that you can be happy only when you are the first—that is sheer nonsense. You can't be happy just by being first, and in trying to be first you go through such misery that by the time you become the first you are habituated to misery.

By the time you become the president or the prime minister of a country you have gone through such misery that now misery is your second nature. You don't know now any other way to exist; you remain miserable. Tension has become ingrained; anxiety has become your way of life. You don't know any other way; this is your very lifestyle. So even though you have become the first, you remain cautious, anxious, afraid. It does not change your inner quality at all.

A real education will not teach you to be the first. It will tell you to enjoy whatever you are doing, not for the result, but for the act itself. Just like a painter or a dancer or a musician . . .

You can paint in two ways. You can paint to compete with other painters; you want to be the greatest painter in the world, you want to be a Picasso or a Van Gogh. Then your painting will be second-rate, because your mind is not interested in painting itself; it is interested in being the first, the greatest painter in the world. You are not going deep into the art of painting. You are not enjoying it, you are only using it as a stepping-stone. You are on an ego trip, and the problem is that to really be a painter, you have to drop the ego completely. To really be a painter, the ego has to be put aside. Only then can existence flow through you. Only then can your hands and your fingers and your brush be used as vehicles. Only then can something of superb beauty be born.

> Ego cannot bring anything extraordinary into the world, the extraordinary comes only through egolessness.

Real beauty is never created by you but only through you. Existence flows; you become only a passage. You allow it to happen, that's all; you don't hinder it, that's all.

But if you are too interested in the result, the ultimate result—that you have to become famous, that you have to be the best painter in the world, that you have to defeat all other painters hitherto—then your interest is not in painting; painting is secondary. And of course, with a secondary interest in painting you can't paint something original; it will be ordinary.

Ego cannot bring anything extraordinary into the world; the extraordinary comes only through egolessness. And so is the case with the musician and the poet and the dancer. So is the case with everybody.

In the *Bhagavad Gita*, Krishna says: Don't think of the result at all. It is a message of tremendous beauty and significance and truth. Don't think of the result at all. Just do what you are doing with your totality. Get lost in it, lose the doer in the doing. Don't "be"—let your creative energies flow unhindered. That's why he said to Arjuna: "Don't escape from the war . . . because I can see this escape is just an ego trip. The way you are talking simply shows that you are calculating, you are thinking that by escaping from the war you will become a great saint. Rather than surrendering to the whole, you are taking yourself too seriously—as if there will be no war if you are not there."

Krishna says to Arjuna, "Just be in a state of let-go. Say to existence, 'Use me in whatever way you want to use me. I am available, unconditionally available.' Then whatsoever happens through you will have a great authenticity about it. It will have intensity, it will have depth. It will have the impact of the eternal on it."

Jesus says: Remember, those who are first in this world will be the last in the kingdom of God, and those who are the last will be the first. He has given you the fundamental law—he has given you the inexhaustible, eternal law: Stop trying to be the first. But remember one thing, which is very much possible, because the mind is so cunning it can distort every truth. You can start trying to be the last—but then you miss the whole point. Then another competition starts: "I have to be the last"—and if somebody else says, "I am the last," then the struggle, the conflict, begins again.

I have heard a Sufi parable:

A great emperor, Nadirshah, was praying. It was early morning; the sun had not yet risen, it was still dark. Nadirshah was about to start the conquest of a new country, and of course he was praying to God for his blessings, to be victorious. He was saying to God, "I am nobody,

I am just a servant—a servant of your servants. Bless me. I am going on your behalf, this is your victory. But I am nobody, remember. I am just a servant of your servants."

A priest was also by his side, helping him in prayer, functioning as a mediator between him and God. And then suddenly they heard another voice in the darkness. A beggar of the town was also praying, and he was saying to God, "I am nobody, a servant of your servants."

The king said, "Look at this beggar! He is a beggar and saying to God that he is nobody! Stop this nonsense! Who are you to say you are nobody? *I* am nobody, and nobody else can claim this. *I* am the servant of God's servants— who are you to say that you are the servant of his servants?"

Now you see? The competition is still there, the same competition, the same stupidity. Nothing has changed. The same calculation: "I have to be the last. Nobody else can be allowed to be the last." The mind can go on playing such games on you if you are not very understanding, if you are not very intelligent.

Never try to be happy at the expense of another man's happiness. That is ugly, inhuman. That is violence in the true sense. If you think you become a saint by condemning others as sinners, your saintliness is nothing but a new ego trip. If you think you are holy because you are trying to prove others unholy . . . That's what your holy people are doing. They go on bragging about their holiness, saintliness. Go to your so-called saints and look into their eyes. They have such condemnation for you! They are saying that you are all bound for hell; they go on condemning everybody. Listen to their sermons; all their sermons are condemnatory. And of course you listen silently to their condemnations because you know that you have made many mistakes in your life, errors in your life. And they have condemned *everything*—so it is impossible to feel that you can be good. You love food, you are a sinner. You don't get up early in the morning, you are a sinner; you don't go to bed early in the evening, you are a sinner. They have arranged everything in such a way that it is very difficult not to be a sinner.

Yes, *they* are not sinners. They go early to bed and they get up early in the morning . . . in fact, they have nothing else to do! They never commit any mistakes because they never do anything. They are just sitting there almost dead. But if you do something, of course, how can you be holy? Hence for centuries the holy man has been renouncing the world and escaping from the world, because to be in the world and be holy seems to be impossible.

My whole approach is that unless you are in the world, your holiness is of no value at all. Be in the world and be holy! We have to define holiness in a totally different way. Don't live at the expense of others' pleasures—that is holiness. Don't destroy others' happiness, help others to be happy—that is holiness. Create the climate in which everybody can have a little joy.

IN PURSUIT

If you are in pursuit of happiness one thing is certain: You are not going to get it. Happiness is always a by-product. It is not the result of a direct pursuit.

THE FUNDAMENTAL DUALITY

The most important question of all questions is: What is true happiness? And is there a possibility to achieve it? Is true happiness possible at all, or is all momentary? Is life only a dream, or is there something substantial in it too? Does life begin with birth and end with death, or is there something that transcends birth and death? Because without the eternal there is no possibility of true happiness. With the momentary, happiness will remain fleeting: One moment it is here, the other moment gone, and you are left in great despair and darkness.

That's how it is in ordinary life, in the life of the unawakened. There are moments of bliss and there are moments of misery; it is all mixed, a hodgepodge. You cannot keep those moments of happiness that come to you. They come on their own and they disappear on their own; you are not the master. And you cannot avoid the moments of misery; they too have their own persistence. They come on their own and they go on their own; you are simply a victim. And between these two—happiness and unhappiness—you are torn apart. You are never left at ease.

This being torn apart into all kinds of dualities . . . The duality of happiness and unhappiness is the most fundamental and the most symptomatic, but there are a thousand and one dualities: the duality of love and hate, the duality of life and death, day and night, summer and winter, youth and old age, and so on, so forth. But the fundamental duality, the duality that represents all other dualities, is that of happiness and unhappiness. And you are torn apart, pulled into different, polar-opposite directions. You cannot be at ease: You are in a dis-ease.

According to the buddhas man is a disease. Is this disease absolute—or can it be transcended?

Hence the basic and the most fundamental question is: What is true happiness? Certainly the happiness that we know is not true; it is dream stuff and it always turns into its own opposite. What looks like happiness one moment turns into unhappiness the next.

Happiness turning into unhappiness simply shows that the two are not separate—maybe two aspects of the same coin. And if you have one side of the coin, the other is always there hidden behind it, waiting for its opportunity to assert—and you know it. When you are happy, deep down somewhere is the lurking fear that it is not going to last, that sooner or later it will be gone, that the night is descending, that any moment you will be engulfed in darkness, that this light is just imaginary—it can't help you, it can't take you to the other shore.

Your happiness is not really happiness but only a hidden unhappiness. Your love is not love but only a mask for your hate. Your compassion is nothing but your anger—cultivated, sophisticated, educated, cultured, civilized, but your compassion is nothing else than anger. Your sensitivity is not real sensitivity but only a mental exercise, a certain attitude and approach practiced.

Remember: The whole of humanity is being brought up with the idea that virtue can be practiced, that goodness can be practiced, that one can learn how to be happy, that one can manage to be happy, that it is within one's power to create a certain character which brings happiness. And that is all wrong, utterly wrong.

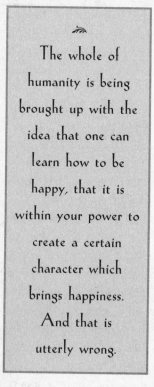

The whole of humanity is being brought up with the idea that one can learn how to be happy, that it is within your power to create a certain character which brings happiness. And that is utterly wrong.

The first thing to be understood about happiness is that it cannot be practiced. It has only to be allowed, because it is not something that you create. Whatsoever *you* create is going to remain something smaller than you, tinier than you. What you create cannot be bigger than you. The painting cannot be bigger than the painter himself and the poetry cannot be bigger than the poet. Your song is bound to be something smaller than you.

If you practice happiness you will be always there at the back, with all your stupidities, with all your ego trips, with all your ignorance, with all your chaos of the mind. With this chaotic mind you cannot create a cosmos, you cannot create grace. Grace always descends from the beyond; it has to be received as a gift in tremendous trust, in total surrender. In a state of let-go true happiness happens.

But we have been told to achieve, to be ambitious. Our mind has been cultivated to be that of an achiever. Our education, culture, religion, they all depend on this basic idea that man has to be ambitious; only the ambitious man will be able to attain fulfillment.

It has never happened, it will never happen, but so deep is the ignorance that we go on believing in this nonsense.

No ambitious person has ever been happy; in fact, the ambitious person is the unhappiest in the world. But we go on training children to be ambitious: "Be the first, be at the top, and you will be happy!" And have you ever seen anybody at the top and happy at the same time? Was Alexander the Great happy when he became a world conqueror? He was one of the unhappiest men who has ever lived on the earth. Seeing the blissfulness of Diogenes, he became jealous. Becoming jealous of a beggar . . .?

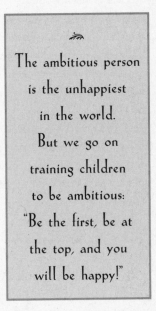

The ambitious person is the unhappiest in the world. But we go on training children to be ambitious: "Be the first, be at the top, and you will be happy!"

Diogenes was a beggar; he had nothing, not even a begging bowl. At least Buddha had a begging bowl with him and three robes. Diogenes was naked—and with no begging bowl. He was going to the river one day with his begging bowl. He was thirsty, it was hot, and he wanted to drink water. And then on the way, just when he was on the bank, a dog passed by him, running, panting, jumped into the river, had a good bath and drank to his heart's content. The idea arose in Diogenes' mind: "This dog is freer than me—he does not have to carry a begging bowl. And if he can manage, why can't I manage without a begging bowl? This is my only possession, and I have to keep an eye on it because it can be stolen. Even in the night once or twice I have to feel whether it is still there or gone." He threw the begging bowl into the river, bowed to the dog, thanked him for the great message that he had brought for him from existence.

This man, who had nothing, created jealousy in Alexander's mind. How miserable he must have been! He confessed to Diogenes, "If ever again God gives me birth, I will ask him, 'This time, please don't make me Alexander—make me Diogenes.'"

Diogenes laughed uproariously, and he called the dog—because they had become friends by now, they had started living together—he called the dog and he said, "Look, listen, what nonsense he is talking about! Next life he wants to be Diogenes! Why next life? Why postpone? Who knows about the next life? Even the next day is uncertain, the next moment is not certain—what to say about the next life! If you really want to be a Diogenes, you can be one right this moment, here now. Throw your clothes into the river and forget all about conquering the world! That is sheer stupidity and you know it.

"And you have confessed that you are miserable, you have confessed that Diogenes is in a far better, more blissful state. So why not be a Diogenes right now? Lie down on the bank of the river where I am taking my sunbath! This bank is big enough for both of us."

Alexander could not accept the invitation, of course. He said, "Thank you for your invitation. Right now I cannot do it, but next life . . ."

Diogenes asked him, "Where are you going? And what will you do even if you have conquered the world?"

Alexander said, "Then I will rest."

Diogenes said, "This seems to be absolutely absurd—because I am resting right now!"

If Alexander is not happy, if Adolf Hitler is not happy, if Rockefellers and Carnegies are not happy—the people who have all the money of the world, if they are not happy, the people who have all the power in the world, if they are not happy . . . Just watch people who have succeeded in the world and you will drop the idea of success. Nothing fails like success. Although you have been told that nothing succeeds like success, I say to you that nothing fails like success.

Happiness has nothing to do with success. Happiness has nothing to do with ambition, happiness has nothing to do with money, power, prestige. It is a totally different dimension. Happiness has something to do with your consciousness, not with your character. Let me remind you—character is not you, it is something you have cultivated. You can become a saint, and still you will not be happy if your sainthood is nothing but a practiced sainthood. And that's how people become

> ‎
> Although you have been told that nothing succeeds like success, I say to you that nothing fails like success. Happiness has nothing to do with success.

saints. Catholics, Jains, Hindus—how do they become saints? They practice inch by inch, in detail, when to get up, what to eat, what not to eat, when to go to bed . . .

NOT CHARACTER BUT CONSCIOUSNESS

I don't believe in character at all. My trust is in consciousness. If a person becomes more conscious, naturally his character is transformed. But that transformation is totally different: it is not managed by the mind—it is natural, it is spontaneous. And whenever your character is natural and spontaneous it has a beauty of its own; otherwise you can go on changing . . . you can drop your anger, but where will you drop it? You will have to drop it within your own unconscious. You can change one side of your life, but whatsoever you throw in will start expressing itself from some other corner. It is bound to be so. You can block a stream with a rock; it will start flowing from somewhere else—you cannot destroy it. Anger is there because you are unconscious, greed is there because you are unconscious, possessiveness and jealousy are there because you are unconscious.

So I am not interested in changing your anger; that will be like pruning leaves of a tree and hoping that the tree will disappear one day. It is not going to be so; on the contrary, the more you prune the tree the thicker will be the foliage.

Hence your so-called saints are the unholiest persons in the world, pretenders, pseudo. Yes, if you look from the outside they look very holy—much too holy, saccharine, too sweet, sickeningly sweet, nauseating. You can only go and pay your respects to them and escape. You can't live with your saints even for twenty-four hours—they will bore you to death! The closer you are to them, the more puzzled, perplexed, confused you will be, because you will start seeing that from one side they have forced away anger, but it has entered into another side of their life.

Ordinary people are angry once in a while, and their anger is very fleeting, very momentary. Then again they are laughing, again they are friendly; they don't carry wounds too long. But your so-called saints, their anger becomes almost a permanent affair. They are simply angry, and not at anything in particular. They have repressed anger so much that now they are simply angry, in a state of rage. Their eyes will show it, their noses will show it, their faces, their very way of life will show it.

Lu Ting ate at a Greek restaurant because Papadopoulos, the owner, made really good fried rice. Each evening he would come in and order "flied lice." This always caused Papadopoulos to fall down with laughter. Sometimes he would have two or three friends standing nearby just to hear Lu Ting order his "flied lice."

Eventually the Chinese's pride was so hurt that he took a special diction lesson just to be able to say "fried rice" correctly.

The next time he went to the restaurant he said very plainly, "Fried rice, please."

Unable to believe his ears, Papadopoulos asked, "What did you say?"

Lu Ting shouted, "You heard what I said, you Gleek plick!"

It won't make much difference—from "flied lice" now it is "Gleek plick"! You close one door, another immediately opens. This is not the way of transformation.

To change your character is easy; the real work consists in changing your consciousness, in becoming conscious—more conscious, more intensely and passionately conscious. When you are conscious it is impossible to be angry, it is impossible to be greedy, it is impossible to be jealous, it is impossible to be ambitious.

And when all anger, greed, ambition, jealousy, possessiveness, lust, disappear the energy involved in them is released. That energy becomes your bliss. Now it is not coming from outside; now it is happening inside your being, in your innermost recesses of being.

And when this energy is available you become a receptive field, you become a magnetic field. You attract

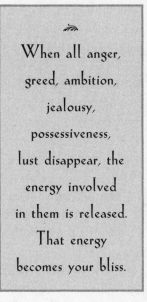

When all anger, greed, ambition, jealousy, possessiveness, lust disappear, the energy involved in them is released. That energy becomes your bliss.

the beyond—when you become a magnetic field, when all the energy that is unnecessarily being wasted by you in your unconsciousness gathers, pools inside you. When you become a lake of energy, you start attracting the stars, you start attracting the beyond, you start attracting paradise itself.

And the meeting of your consciousness with the beyond is the point of bliss, true happiness. It knows nothing of unhappiness, it is pure happiness. It knows nothing of death, it is pure life. It knows nothing of darkness, it is pure light, and to know it is the goal. Gautama the Buddha went in search of this and one day, after six years' struggle, he attained it.

You can also attain it, but let me remind you: By saying that you can attain it I am not creating a desire to attain it. I am simply stating a fact: that if you become a pool of immense energy, undistracted by any worldly thing, it happens. It is more a happening than a doing. And it is better to call it bliss than happiness, because the word *happiness* makes you think it is similar to what you know as happiness. What you know as happiness is nothing but a relative state.

> Benson went to Krantz's clothing store to buy himself a suit. He found just the style he wanted, so he took the jacket off the hanger and tried it on.
>
> Krantz came up to him. "Yes, sir. It looks wonderful on you."
>
> "It may look wonderful," said Benson, "but it fits terrible. The shoulders pinch."
>
> "Put on the pants," said Krantz. "They are so tight, you will forget all about the shoulders!"

What you call happiness is just a question of relativity. What the buddhas call happiness is something absolute. Your happiness is a relative phenomenon. What the buddhas call happiness is something absolute, unrelated to anybody else. It is not in comparison with somebody else; it is simply yours, it is inner.

CHASING RAINBOWS

The American Constitution contains a very stupid idea. It says that the pursuit of happiness is man's birthright. The people who wrote this constitution had no idea what they were writing. If the pursuit of happiness is the birthright of mankind, then what about unhappiness? Whose birthright is unhappiness? These people were not at all aware that if you ask for happiness, you have asked for unhappiness at the same time; whether you know it or not does not matter.

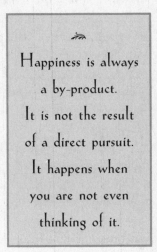

Happiness is always a by-product. It is not the result of a direct pursuit. It happens when you are not even thinking of it.

I call it stupid because nobody can be in pursuit of happiness. And if you are in pursuit of happiness one thing is certain: You are not going to get it. Happiness is always a by-product. It is not the result of a direct pursuit. It happens when you are not even thinking of it—what to say of pursuit? It happens suddenly, out of nowhere. You were doing something totally different.

You may be chopping wood—certainly it is not the pursuit of happiness, chopping wood, but in the early morning sun when it is still cool, the noise of your axe falling on the wood . . . pieces of wood being thrown all around, making a noise and then leaving a silence behind . . . You start perspiring, and the cool breeze makes you feel even cooler than before. Suddenly there is happiness, a joy uncontainable. But you were simply chopping wood—and chopping wood is not mentioned as a birthright in the constitution, because then, how many things are you going to include?

I cannot forget one day . . . There are a few things that make no logical sense and have no relevance but somehow remain hanging in your memory. You cannot understand for what reason they are there because millions of things have happened far more important, far more significant, and they have all disappeared. But a few insignificant things have left a trace behind; you cannot find any reason why, but they have remained.

One such thing I remember. I was coming home from school—my school was almost a mile away from my home. Just halfway there was a huge bo tree. I passed that bo tree every day at least four times: going to school, then in the middle of the day coming home for lunch, then going to school again, then coming back home. So many thousands of times I had passed that tree, but one day something happened.

It was a hot day, and as I came close to the tree, I was perspiring. I passed under the tree and it was so cool that without having any deliberate thought I stopped for a while, not knowing why. I simply went close to the tree trunk, sat there and felt the tree trunk. I cannot explain what happened but I felt so immensely happy, as if something was transpiring between me and the tree. The coolness could not be the cause, because many times when I had been perspiring, I had passed through the coolness of the tree. I had also stopped before, but never before had I gone and touched the tree and sat there as if meeting an old friend.

That moment has remained shining like a star. So much has happened in my life, but I don't see that moment diminishing in any way: it is still there. Whenever I look back it is still there. That day I was not clearly aware what had happened nor can I say today—but something happened. And from that day I had a certain relatedness with the tree which I had not felt before, even with any human being. I became more intimate with that tree than with anybody else in the whole world. It became a routine for me: Whenever I passed the tree, I would sit for a few seconds or a few minutes and just feel the tree. I can still see it—something went on growing between us.

The day I left school and moved to another city to enter the university, I took leave of my father, of my mother, of my uncles and my whole family, without weeping. I was never the type who easily cries or weeps. But on that same day, taking leave of the bo tree, I wept. It remains a very lighted spot. And when I was crying I had an absolute certainty that there were tears in the eyes of the tree too, although I could not see the eyes of the tree, and I could not see the tears. But I could feel—when I touched the tree I could feel the sadness, and I could feel a blessing, a good-bye. And it was certainly my last meeting, because when I came back after one year, for some stupid reason the tree had been cut down and removed.

The stupid reason was that they were making a small memorial pillar, and that was the most beautiful spot in the middle of the city. It was for an idiot who was rich enough to win all the elections and become the president of the municipal committee. He had been president for at least thirty-five years—the longest time anybody had been president in the town. Everybody was happy with his presidency because he was such an idiot; you could do anything and he was not going to create any interference. You could build your house in the middle of the street, he would not bother you; you just had to vote for him. So the whole town was happy with him because everybody had such freedom. The municipal committee, the members, the clerks and the head clerks—all were happy with him. Everybody wanted him to remain eternally the president; but even idiots have to die, fortunately. But his death was unfortunate because they looked for a place to make a memorial for him, and they destroyed the bo tree. Now his marble stone stands there instead of a living tree.

The pursuit of happiness is an impossible thing. If you look at your own experience and find moments when you were happy—which are bound to be very rare—perhaps in a life of seventy years you may have seven moments which you can claim as moments of happiness. But if you had even a single moment of happiness, one thing is certain without any exception: It happened when you were not looking for it.

Try to look for happiness, and you are certain to miss it.

I disagree with Jesus Christ on many points, even on points that look very innocent, and it looks as if I am being unkind. Jesus says: "Seek, and ye shall find. Ask, and it shall be given to you. Knock, and the doors shall be opened unto you." I cannot agree.

The fools who wrote the American Constitution were certainly influenced by Jesus Christ, of course—they were all Christians. When they said "the pursuit of happiness," they must have consciously or unconsciously had in mind the statement of Jesus: "Seek, and ye shall find." But I say to you: Seek, and be certain you shall never find it. Seek not, and it is there.

Just stop seeking, and you have found it—because seeking means an effort of the mind, and nonseeking means a state of relaxation. And happiness is possible only when you are relaxed.

A seeker is not relaxed. How can he be relaxed? He cannot afford relaxation. You will be surprised if you look around in the world: you will find people in very poor countries more contented than those in rich ones. Yes, even in Ethiopia where they are dying of starvation, you will find people who are dying but who are not suffering or in anguish. The greatest number of unhappy people you will find in America. This is strange. In America, the pursuit of happiness is a birthright. It is not mentioned in any other constitution in the world.

This American Constitution is absolutely insane. "Pursuit of happiness"? Nobody has ever succeeded in it, and those who have tried have become very unhappy and miserable in their lives.

Happiness *happens*. Perhaps that's why you call it "happiness"—

because it *happens*. You cannot manage it, you cannot manufacture it, you cannot arrange it. Happiness is something that is beyond your effort, beyond you. But just by digging a hole in your garden, if you are totally absorbed in it—if the whole world is forgotten, including you—it is there.

Happiness is always with you. It has nothing to do with the weather, it has nothing to do with chopping wood, it has nothing to do with digging a hole in the garden. Happiness has nothing to do with anything. It is just the nonexpectant, relaxed, at-ease state of your being with existence. And it is there; it does not come and go. It is always there, just like your breathing, your heartbeat, the blood circulating in your body.

Happiness is always there, but if you seek it you will find unhappiness. By seeking you will miss happiness—that's what unhappiness is, missing happiness. Unhappiness has a certain relationship with pursuit, a partnership. If you "pursue," you will find unhappiness. And the American Constitution has given the idea to all the American people that they should "pursue."

And they are pursuing desperately—for money, power, religion—and they are running all over the world looking for somebody to teach them how to find happiness.

The thing to do is to just come back home and forget all about it. Do something that has nothing to do with happiness. Paint. You need not learn painting; can't you throw color on a canvas? Any child can do it. Just throw colors on a canvas and you may be surprised: You are not a painter, but something beautiful happens. Just the colors themselves have become mixed in a certain way and have created something that you cannot name.

Modern paintings are without titles, and many paintings are even without frames because existence has no frame. You look from your window—you see the sky framed, but the frame exists in the window, not in the sky; the sky has no frame. So there are painters who don't even paint on a canvas; they paint on the walls, on the floors, on the ceilings. Strange places—but I can see their insight. They are not interested in making a painting; they are more interested in getting involved in the very act of painting. It is not for sale. How can you sell your ceiling, and who is going to buy it? But while they are so absorbed, from some unknown corner something starts slipping into their being. They start feeling joyous for no reason at all.

That's why I condemn the idea of pursuit. About whoever wrote this word *pursuit* into the Constitution, I can say without knowing his name, without knowing anything about him, that he must have been an utterly miserable man. He had never known happiness. He had been *pursuing* it; hence, he tried to give every American the same birthright that he had claimed for himself. And nobody has criticized it in three hundred years, such a simple thing.

A poet, a painter, a singer, a dancer, yes, once in a while attain happiness. But one thing is always part of it: Whenever happiness comes, *they* are not there. The pursuer is not there, the pursuit is not there.

Nijinsky, one of the most significant dancers in the world, in the whole of history . . . As far as I am concerned, he is the best dancer humanity has ever produced. He was a miracle when he danced. Once in a while he would take such a big leap that it defied gravity; it was not possible, scientifically it was impossible. Such a huge, high leap was absolutely impossible according to the laws of gravity. Even the people who compete in the Olympic long jumps are nothing compared to Nijinsky when he used to jump. And even more miraculous was his coming back down: He came back like a feather, slowly. That went even more against the laws of gravity, because gravity would pull the weight of a human body suddenly, quickly. You would fall with a thump, you might even get a few fractures! But he used to come down just the way a dead leaf falls from the tree: slowly, lazily, in no hurry, because there is nowhere to reach. Or even better, featherlike, because a leaf comes down a little faster. The feather of a bird is lightweight, very light-weight; it comes down dancing. In that same way Nijinsky used to come back down. There was not even a sound when he landed on the stage.

He was asked again and again, "How do you do it?"

He said, "I don't do it. I have tried to do it, but whenever I have tried, it has not happened. The more I have tried, the more it was clear to me that it is not something I can manage. Slowly, slowly, I became aware that it happens when I don't try, when I am not even thinking of it. When I am not even there, suddenly I find it is there, it is happening. And by the time I am back to figure out how it happened, it is no longer there, already gone, and I am back on the floor."

Now, this man knows happiness cannot be pursued. If Nijinsky had been on the panel writing the Constitution of America, he would have objected and said that *pursuit* is absolutely the wrong word. Simply say that happiness is everybody's birthright, not its pursuit. It is not like a hunter pursuing game. Then you will run your whole life, chasing shadows and never arriving anywhere. Your whole life will pass by as sheer wastage.

But the American mind has this idea, so in every sphere—politics, business, religion—they are pursuing. The Americans are always on the go, and going fast, because when you are going then why not go fast? And don't ask where you are going, because nobody knows. One thing is certain, they are going at full speed, with as much speed as they can maintain, all that they can manage. What more is needed? You are going, you are going at full speed. You are fulfilling your birthright.

So people are passing from one woman to another woman, to another woman, to another woman; from one man, to another man, to another man; from one business to another business, from one job to another job—all in the pursuit of happiness. And strangely, it always looks as if happiness is there and somebody else is enjoying it, so you start pursuing it. When you reach where you think you are going to find it, it is not there.

The grass beyond your fence is always greener, but don't jump the fence to see whether it is actually so. Enjoy it! If it is greener on the other side of the fence, enjoy it. Why destroy things by jumping the fence and finding out that it is worse than your own grass?

But people are running after everything, thinking that perhaps this will give them what they have been missing.

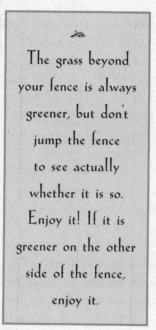

The grass beyond your fence is always greener, but don't jump the fence to see actually whether it is so. Enjoy it! If it is greener on the other side of the fence, enjoy it.

Nothing will help. You can live in a palace but you will be just as miserable, perhaps more than you were in an old hut. In the old hut at least there was the consolation that you were miserable because you were in an old, rotten hut. There was an excuse; you could have explained away your miserliness, your misery, your suffering. And there was also a hope that someday you would be able to manage a better house—if not a palace, then at least a good, beautiful, small house of your own.

It is hope that is keeping people alive, and it is their excuses and explanations that keep them trying again and again. It has become the philosophy of America to try, try, and try again. But there are a few things that are not achievable within the realm of trying, which happen only when you are completely finished with trying. You simply sit down and you say, "Enough is enough—I am not going to try."

That's how enlightenment happened to Gautam Buddha.

He must have been the first American, because he was in pursuit of happiness. Because of the pursuit, he dropped his kingdom. He is a pioneer in many things; he is the first dropout. Your hippies have not dropped much. To drop something, first you have to have it. He had it, and he had it more than any man ever had it. Buddha was surrounded by all the beautiful women from the kingdom. So no desire remained unfulfilled: He had the best of food, hundreds of servants, huge gardens.

Buddha said, "I am renouncing it all. I have not found happiness here. I will seek it, I will pursue it, I will do everything that is needed to find happiness."

And for six years Buddha did everything that anybody can do. He went to all kinds of teachers, masters, scholars, wisemen, sages, saints. And India is so full of these people that you need not seek and search; you simply move anywhere and you meet them. They are all over the place; if you don't seek them, they will seek you. And particularly in Buddha's time it was really at a peak. But after six years' tremendous effort—austerities, fasting, and yoga postures— nothing happened. And one day . . .

Niranjana is a small river, not very deep. Buddha was fasting and practicing austerities and torturing himself in every way, and he had become so weak that when he went for a bath in the Niranjana he could not cross the river. The river was small, but he was so weak that only by holding on to a root of a tree, which was hanging by the side of the bank, could he manage to keep himself there; otherwise the river would take him away. While he was hanging on to the root, the idea occurred to him: "These sages say that existence is like an ocean. If existence is an ocean, then whatever I am doing is not right, because if I can't cross this poor river, Niranjana, how am I going to cross the ocean of existence? Whatever I have been doing, I have simply wasted my time, my life, my energy, my body." Somehow he managed to come out of the river, and he dropped all effort and sat under the tree.

That evening—it was a full-moon night—for the first time in

six years he slept well, because there was nothing to do the next day, nowhere to go. No practice, no exercise . . . the next day there was no need even to get up in the early morning before sunrise. The next day he could sleep as much he wanted. For the first time he felt a total freedom from all effort, seeking, search, pursuit.

Of course he slept in a tremendously relaxed way, and in the morning, as he opened his eyes, the last star was disappearing. It is said, with the last star disappearing, Buddha disappeared too. The whole night's rest, peace, no future, no goal, nothing to be done . . . for the first time he was not an American. Lying down, in no hurry even to get up, he simply saw that all those six years looked like a nightmare. But it was past. The star disappeared, and Siddhartha disappeared.

This was the experience of bliss, or truth; of transcendence, of all that you have been seeking but you have been missing because you have been seeking. Even Buddhists have not been able to understand the significance of this story. This is the most important story in Gautam Buddha's life. Nothing else is comparable to it.

But you will be surprised . . . I am not a Buddhist and I don't agree with Buddha on a thousand and one things, but I am the first man in twenty-five centuries who has put emphasis on this story and made it the central focus, because this is where Buddha's awakening happened. But Buddhist priests and monks cannot even tell this story, because if they tell this story, what purpose do they have? What are they doing? What are they teaching, what exercises, what prayers? Naturally, if you tell this story, that it happened when Buddha stopped doing all kinds of religious nonsense, people will say, "Then why are you teaching us to do religious nonsense? Just to drop it someday? And if we have to drop it finally, why begin in the first place?"

It will be difficult to convince the priests; their whole business and their whole profession will be destroyed.

Bliss also showers exactly like that. Truth also showers exactly like that. You just have to be sitting, doing nothing, waiting—not waiting for Godot, just waiting; not for anything in particular but simply waiting, in a state of awaiting, and it happens.

And because it *happens*, it is perfectly right to call it happiness.

THE ROOTS OF MISERY

Man is in misery, and man has remained in misery down the centuries. Rarely can you find a human being who is not miserable. It is so rare that it almost seems unbelievable. That's why people don't believe that human beings like Buddha ever existed. People can't believe it—they can't believe it because of their own misery. The misery is such, and they are entangled in it so deeply, that they don't see that any escape could be possible.

People think the buddhas must have been imagined, that people like Gautam Buddha are dreams of humanity. That's what Sigmund Freud says, that people like Buddha are "wish fulfillments." We want to be that way, we want to be out of misery, we would like to have that silence, that peace, that benediction—but it has not happened. And Freud says there is no hope; it *cannot* happen, by the very nature of things. Man cannot become happy.

Freud has to be listened to very keenly and very deeply; he cannot be simply rejected outright. His is one of the most penetrating minds ever, and when he says happiness is not possible, when he says that hoping for happiness is hoping for the impossible, he means it. This conclusion is not that of a philosopher. His own observation of human misery led him to this conclusion. Freud is not a pessimist, but after observing thousands of human beings, getting deeper into their psyches, he realized that man is made in such a way that he has a built-in process for being miserable. At the most he can be in comfort, but never in ecstasy. At the most we can make life a little more convenient—through scientific technology, through social change, through a better economy, and other things—but man will remain miserable all the same. How can Freud believe that a person like Buddha ever existed? Such serenity seems to be just a dream; humanity has been dreaming about Buddha.

This idea arises because Buddha is so rare, so exceptional. He is not the rule.

Why has man remained in so much misery? And the miracle is that everybody *wants* to be happy. You cannot find a single person who *wants* to be miserable, yet everybody is in misery. Everybody wants to be happy, blissful, peaceful, silent. Everybody wants to be in joy, everybody wants to celebrate—but it seems impossible. Now there must be some very deep cause, so deep that Freudian analysis could not reach it, so deep that logic cannot penetrate it.

One basic thing has to be understood. Man wants happiness; that's why he is miserable. The more you want to be happy, the more miserable you will be. Now this seems very absurd, but this is the root cause. And when you understand the process of how the human mind functions you will be able to realize it.

Man wants to be happy; hence he creates misery. If you want to get out of misery, you will have to get out of your desire for happiness—then nobody can make you miserable. Here is what Freud missed. He could not understand that the very desire for happiness can be the cause of misery.

How does it happen? Why in the first place do you desire happiness? And what does the desire for happiness do to you?

The moment you desire happiness, you have moved away from the present. You have moved away from the existential, you have already moved into the future—which is nowhere, which has not come yet. You have moved into a dream. Now, dreams can never be fulfilling. Your desire for happiness is a dream, the dream is unreal. Through the unreal, nobody has ever been able to reach the real. You have taken a wrong train.

The desire for happiness simply shows that you are not happy right at this moment. The desire for happiness simply shows that you are a miserable being. And a miserable being projects into the future that sometime, someday, some way, he will be happy. Your projection comes out of misery; it carries the very seeds of misery. It comes out of you; it cannot be different from you. It is your child—its face will be like you; your blood will be circulating in its body. It will be your continuity.

You are unhappy today. You project that tomorrow will be happy, but tomorrow is a projection of you, of whatever you are today. You are unhappy—the tomorrow will come out of this unhappiness and you will be more unhappy. Of course, out of more unhappiness you will again desire happiness in the future. Then you are caught in a vicious circle: the more unhappy you become, the more you desire happiness; the more you desire happiness, the more unhappy you become. Now it is like a dog chasing its own tail.

In Zen they have a certain phrase for it. They say it's like whipping the cart. If your horses are not moving and you go on whipping the cart, it is not going to help. You are miserable, then anything you can dream, anything you can project, is going to bring more misery.

So the first thing is not to dream, not to project. The first thing is to be here now. Whatsoever it is, just be here now—and a tremendous revelation is waiting for you.

The revelation is that nobody can be unhappy in the here and now.

Have you ever been unhappy here and now? Right this moment—is there any possibility of being unhappy *right now*? You can think about yesterday and you can become unhappy. You can think about tomorrow and you can become unhappy. But *right this very moment*—this throbbing, beating, real moment—can you be unhappy right now? Without any past, without any future?

You can bring misery from the past, from your memory. Somebody insulted you yesterday and you can still carry the wound, you can still carry the hurt, and you can still feel unhappy about it: Why—why did it happen to you? Why did the man insult you? You have been doing so much good for him, and you have always been helpful, always a friend—and he insulted you! You are playing with something that exists no longer. Yesterday is gone.

Or you can be unhappy for tomorrow. Tomorrow your money will be finished—then where are you going to stay? What are you going to eat? Tomorrow your money will be finished—then unhappiness arrives. Either it comes from yesterday or it comes from tomorrow, but it is never here and now. Right this moment, in the now, unhappiness is impossible.

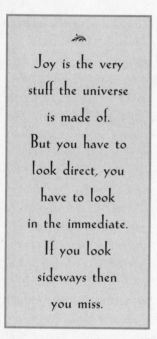

Joy is the very stuff the universe is made of. But you have to look direct, you have to look in the immediate. If you look sideways then you miss.

If you have learned this much, you can become a buddha. Then nobody is hindering your path. Then you can forget all the Freuds; then happiness is not only possible, it has already happened. It is just in front of you and you are missing it because you go on looking sideways.

Happiness is where you are— wherever you are, happiness is there. It surrounds you, it is a natural phenomenon. It is just like air, just like sky. Happiness is not to be sought, it is the very stuff the universe is made of. Joy is the very stuff the universe is made of. But you have to look straight-on, you have to look in the immediate. If you look sideways then you miss it.

You miss because of yourself. You miss because you have a wrong approach.

But go on dying to the past and never think of the future, and then try to be miserable—you will fail! You cannot be miserable; your failure is absolutely certain, it can be predicted. You cannot manage—however efficient you are at being miserable, however well trained, you cannot create misery *this* very moment.

Desiring happiness helps you to look somewhere else, and then you go on missing. Happiness is not to be created—happiness is just to be *seen*. It is already present. This very moment, you can become happy, tremendously happy.

This is how it happened to Buddha. He was the son of a king, he had everything but was not happy. He became more and more unhappy—the more you have, the more unhappy you become. That is the misery of a rich man. That's what is happening in America today: The richer they get the more unhappy they become; the richer they get the more they are completely at a loss what to do.

Poor people are always certain about what to do: They have to earn money, they have to build a good house, they have to buy a car; they have to send their children to the university. They always have a program waiting for them. They are occupied. They have a future, they have hope: "Someday or other . . ." They remain in misery, but there is hope.

The rich man is in misery and the hope has also disappeared. His misery is double. You cannot find a poorer man than a rich man; he is doubly poor. He remains projected into the future, and now he knows the future is not going to supply anything—because whatever he needs, he already has it. He becomes troubled, his mind becomes more and more anxious, apprehensive. He becomes anguished. That's what happened to Buddha.

He was rich. He had everything that it was possible to have. He became very unhappy. One day he escaped from his palace, left all the riches, his beautiful wife, his newly born child—he escaped. He became a beggar. He started seeking happiness. He went to this guru, to that guru; he asked everybody what to do to be happy— and of course there were a thousand and one people ready to advise him and he followed everybody's advice. And the more he followed their advice, the more confused he became.

Buddha tried whatever was said to him. Somebody said: "Do hatha yoga"; he became a hatha yogi. He did yoga postures and he did them to the very extreme. Nothing came out of it. Maybe you can have a better body with hatha yoga, but you cannot become happy. Just a better body, a healthier body, makes no difference. With more energy you will have more energy at your disposal to become unhappy—but you will become unhappy. What will you do with it? If you have more money, what are you going to do with it? You will do that which you can do, and if a little money makes you so miserable, more money will make you more miserable. It is simple arithmetic.

Buddha dropped all yoga. He went to other teachers, the raja yogis, who teach no body postures but only mantras, chanting, meditations. He did that too, but nothing came out of it. He was *really* in search. When you are really in search then nothing can help, then there is no remedy.

Mediocre people stop somewhere along the way; they are not real seekers. A real seeker is one who goes to the very end of the search, and comes to realize that all search is nonsense. Searching itself is a way of desire—Buddha recognized that one day. He had left his palace, he had left his worldly possessions; one day, after six years of spiritual search, he dropped all search. The material search was dropped before, now he dropped the spiritual search. This world was dropped before, now he dropped the other world too.

He was completely rid of desire . . . and that very moment it happened. That very moment there was benediction. All desire dropped, all hope dropped, all hope abandoned, suddenly Gautam Siddartha became Buddha. It was always there but he was looking somewhere else. It was there—inside, outside, it is how the universe is made. It is blissful, it is truth, it is divine.

FROM AGONY
TO ECSTASY

Joy is to enter into your own self. In the beginning it is difficult, arduous. In the beginning you will have to face misery; the path is very mountainous. But the more you enter into it, the greater is the reward.

UNDERSTANDING IS THE KEY

You have to understand one thing: that enlightenment is not an escape from pain but an understanding of pain, an understanding of your anguish, an understanding of your misery— not a cover-up, not a substitute, but a deep insight: "Why am I miserable, why is there so much anxiety, why is there so much anguish, what are the causes in me that are creating it?" And to see those causes clearly is to be free from them.

Just an insight into your misery brings a freedom from misery. And what remains is enlightenment. Enlightenment is not something that comes to you. It is when pain and misery and anguish and anxiety have been understood perfectly well and they have evaporated because now they have no cause to exist in you—that state is enlightenment. It will bring you, for the first time, real contentment, real blissfulness, authentic ecstasy. And only then can you compare.

What you used to call "contentment" before was not contentment. What you used to call "happiness" before was not happiness. But right now you don't have anything to compare it with.

Once enlightenment gives you a taste of the real, you will see that all your pleasures, all your happinesses, were simply the stuff dreams are made of; they were not real. And what has come now, has come forever.

That is the definition of the real: A contentment that comes and never leaves you again is real contentment. A contentment that comes and goes again is not contentment, it is simply a gap between two miseries. Just as we call a gap between two wars "peacetime"—it is not a peaceful time, it is simply preparation for another war. If the war is a positive war, the time between two wars is a negative war, a cold war. It goes on underground, you are getting ready for a hot war.

Anything that comes and goes is a dream. Let that be the definition. Anything that comes and never goes is reality.

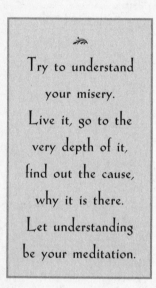

Try to understand your misery. Live it, go to the very depth of it, find out the cause, why it is there. Let understanding be your meditation.

Try to understand your misery. Live it, go to the very depth of it, find out the cause, why it is there. Let understanding be your meditation.

And try to understand your contentment also, your happiness also, and you will see their superficiality. Once you know that your happiness is superficial and your anguish is very deep—and it is in your hands—you can change your whole style of consciousness. Your contentment can become your whole being; not even a small space is left for discontentment.

Your love becomes your very life. And it remains. Time passes, but what you have achieved goes on deepening. More and more flowers, more and more songs are born out of it. That's what we call "enlightenment" The word is Eastern, but the experience has nothing to do with East or West.

BREAD AND CIRCUSES

Ordinarily what we think is joy is not joy; at the most it is entertainment. It is just a way to avoid oneself. It is a way to intoxicate yourself, it is a way to be drowned in something so you can forget your misery, your worry, your anguish, your anxiety.

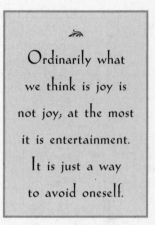

Ordinarily what we think is joy is not joy; at the most it is entertainment. It is just a way to avoid oneself.

So all kinds of entertainments are thought to be joy—they are not! Anything that comes from the outside is not, and cannot be, a joy. Anything that depends on something is not, and cannot be, a joy. Joy arises out of your very core. It is absolutely independent—independent of any outer circumstance. And it is not an escape from oneself; it is really encountering oneself. Joy arises only when you come home.

So whatsoever is known as joy is just the contrary, just the diametrically opposite: it is not joy. In fact because you are joyless you seek entertainment.

It happened that one of the great Russian novelists, Maxim Gorky, visited America. He was shown all kinds of things that Americans have devised to entertain themselves, to get lost in. The man who was directing his tour was hoping that he would be very happy. But the more Maxim Gorky was shown around, the more unhappy and sad he looked.

The guide asked him, "What is the matter? Can't you understand?"

Maxim Gorky said, "I can understand—that's why I am feeling sad. This country must be joyless; otherwise there is no need for so many entertainments."

Only a joyless person needs entertainment. The more joyless the world becomes, the more we need the TV, films, tinsel towns, and a thousand and one things. We need alcohol more and more, we need new kinds of drugs more and more—just to avoid the misery that we are, just not to face the anguish that we are, just somehow to forget it all. But by forgetting it nothing is achieved.

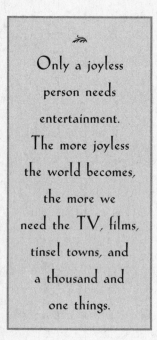

Only a joyless person needs entertainment. The more joyless the world becomes, the more we need the TV, films, tinsel towns, and a thousand and one things.

So joy is to enter into your own self. In the beginning it is difficult, arduous. In the beginning you will have to face misery; the path is very mountainous. But the deeper you enter into it, the greater the payoff, the greater the reward.

Once you have learned how to face your misery, you start becoming joyful, because in the process of facing it the misery starts disappearing and you start becoming more and more integrated.

One day the misery is there and you are facing it—suddenly, the break: You can see the misery as separate from you and you are separate from it. You have always been separate; it was just an illusion, an identification that you got into. Now you know you are not this, and then there is an outburst of joy, an explosion of joy.

ECSTASY IS REBELLIOUS

Every child is born ecstatic. Ecstasy is natural. It is not something that happens only to great sages. It is something that we all bring with us into the world; everybody comes with it. It is life's innermost core. It is part of being alive. Life is ecstasy. Every child brings it into the world, but then the society jumps on the child, starts destroying the possibility of ecstasy, starts making the child miserable, starts conditioning the child.

> You can control only a miserable person. An ecstatic person is bound to be free. Ecstasy is freedom. When you are ecstatic, you cannot be reduced to being a slave.

The society is neurotic, and it cannot allow ecstatic people to be here. They are dangerous for it. Try to understand the mechanism; then things will be easier.

You cannot control an ecstatic person; it is impossible. You can control only a miserable person. An ecstatic person is bound to be free. Ecstasy is freedom. When you are ecstatic, you cannot be reduced to being a slave. You cannot be destroyed so easily; you cannot be persuaded to live in a prison. You would like to dance under the stars and you would like to walk with the wind and you would like to talk with the sun and the moon. You will need the vast, the infinite, the huge, the enormous. You cannot be seduced into living in a dark cell. You cannot be turned into a slave. You will live your own life and you will do your thing.

This is very difficult for the society. If there are many ecstatic people, the society will feel it is falling apart, its structure will not hold anymore. Ecstatic people will be rebels. Remember, I don't call an ecstatic person a "revolutionary"; I call him a "rebel." A revolutionary is one who wants to change the society, but he wants to replace it with another society. A rebel is one who wants to live as an individual and would like there to be no rigid social structure in the world. A rebel is one who does not want to replace this society with another society—because all societies have proved to be the same. The capitalist and the communist and the fascist and the socialist, they are all cousin-brothers; it doesn't make much difference. The society is society. All the churches have proved to be the same—the Hindu, the Christian, the Mohammedan. Once a structure becomes powerful, it does not want anybody to be ecstatic, because ecstasy is against structure.

Listen to it and meditate over it: Ecstasy is against structure. Ecstasy is rebellious. It is not revolutionary. A revolutionary wants another structure—of his own desire, of his own utopia, but a structure all the same. He wants to be in power. He wants to be the oppressor and not the oppressed; he wants to be the exploiter and not the exploited; he wants to rule and not be ruled.

A rebel is one who neither wants to be ruled nor wants to rule. A rebel is one who wants no rule in the world. A rebel is anarchic. A rebel is one who trusts nature, not man-made structures, who trusts that if nature is left alone, everything will be beautiful. It is!

Such a vast universe goes on without any government. Animals, birds, trees, everything goes on without any government. Why does man need government? Something must have gone wrong. Why is man so neurotic that he cannot live without rulers?

Now that is a vicious circle. Man can live without rulers, but he has never been given any opportunity—the rulers won't give you any opportunity. Once you know you can live without rulers, who would want them to be there? Who will support them? Right now you are supporting your own enemies. You go on voting for your own enemies. Two enemies stand against each other in a presidential contest; and you choose. Both are the same. It is as if you are given freedom to choose which prison you want to go into. And you vote happily—I would like to go to prison A or B, I believe in the Republican prison, I believe in the Democratic prison. But both are prisons. And once you support a prison, the prison has its own investment. Then it will not allow you to have a taste of freedom.

> Why does man need government? Something must have gone wrong. Why is man so neurotic that he cannot live without rulers?

So from very childhood we are not allowed to taste freedom, because once we know what freedom is, then we will not concede, we will not compromise—then we will not be ready to live in any dark cell. We would rather die than to allow anybody to reduce us to slavery. We will be assertive.

Of course a rebel will not be interested in becoming powerful over other people. These are signs of neurosis, when you are too interested in becoming powerful over people. That simply shows that deep down you are powerless and you are afraid that if you don't become powerful others are going to overpower you.

Machiavelli says that the best way of defense is to attack.

The best way to protect yourself is to attack first. These so-called politicians all over the world—in the East, in the West—are all deep down very weak people, suffering from inferiority, afraid that if they don't become powerful politically then somebody is going to exploit them, so why not exploit rather than be exploited? The exploited and the exploiter, both are sailing in the same boat—and both are rowing the boat, keeping it afloat.

Once the child knows the taste of freedom, he will never become part of any society, any church, any club, any political party. He will remain an individual, he will remain free and he will create pulsations of freedom around him. His very being will become a door to freedom.

The child is not allowed to taste freedom. If the child asks the mother, "Mom, can I go outside? The sun is beautiful and the air is very crisp and I would like to run around the block," immediately—obsessively, compulsively—the mother says, "No!" The child has not asked much. He just wanted to go out into the morning sun, into the brisk air, he wanted to enjoy the sunlight and the air and the company of the trees—he has not asked for anything!—but out of some deep compulsion, the mother says no. It is very difficult to hear a mother saying yes, very difficult to hear a father saying yes. Even if they say yes, they say it very reluctantly. Even if they say yes, they make the child feel that he is guilty, that he is forcing them, that he is doing something wrong.

Whenever the child feels happy, whatever he is doing, somebody or other is bound to come and stop him—"Don't do this!" By and by the child understands, "Whatever I feel happy about is wrong." And of course he never feels happy doing what others tell him to do, because it is not a spontaneous urge in him. So he comes to know that to be miserable is right, to be happy is wrong. That becomes the deep association.

If he wants to open the clock and look inside, the whole family jumps on him: "Stop! You will destroy the clock. This is not good."

He was just looking into the clock; it was a scientific curiosity. He wanted to see what makes it tick. It was perfectly okay. And the clock is not so valuable as his curiosity, as his inquiring mind. The clock is worthless—even if it is destroyed nothing is destroyed—but once the inquiring mind is destroyed much is destroyed; then he will never inquire for truth.

Or it is a beautiful night and the sky is full of stars and the child wants to sit outside, but it is time to go to sleep. He is not feeling sleepy at all; he is wide awake, very, very much awake. The child is puzzled. In the morning when he feels sleepy, everybody is after him: "Get up!" When he was enjoying it, when it was so beautiful to be in bed, when he wanted to turn over and sleep a little longer and dream a little more, then everybody was against him: "Get up! It is time to get up." Now he is wide-awake and he wants to enjoy the stars. It is very poetic, this moment, very romantic. He feels thrilled. How can he go to sleep in such a state? He is so excited, he wants to sing and dance, and they are forcing him to go to sleep: "It is nine o'clock. It is time to go to sleep." Now, he is happy being awake but he is forced to go to sleep.

When he is playing he is forced to come to the dining table. He is not hungry. When he is hungry, his mother says, "This is not the time." In this way we go on destroying all possibility of being ecstatic, all possibility of being happy, joyful, delighted. What the child feels spontaneously happy with seems to be wrong, and what he does not feel at all interested in seems to be right.

In the school a bird suddenly starts singing outside the classroom, and the child is devoting all his attention toward the bird, of course—not toward the mathematics teacher who is standing at the board with his ugly chalk. But the teacher is more powerful, politically more powerful than the bird. Certainly, the bird has no power, but it has beauty. The bird attracts the child without hammering on his head, "Be attentive! Concentrate on me!" No—simply, spontaneously, naturally, the consciousness of the child starts flowing out the window. It goes to the bird. His heart is there, but he has to look at the blackboard. There is nothing to look at, but he has to pretend.

Happiness is wrong. Wherever there is happiness the child starts becoming afraid something is going to be wrong. If the child is playing with his own body, it is wrong. If the child is playing with his own sexual organs, it is wrong. And that is one of the most ecstatic moments in the life of a child. He enjoys his body; it is thrilling. But all thrill has to be cut, all joy has to be destroyed. It is neurotic, but the society is neurotic.

The same was done to the parents by their parents; they are doing the same to their children. This way one generation goes on destroying another. This way we transfer our neurosis from one generation to another. The whole earth has become a madhouse. Nobody seems to know what ecstasy is. It is lost. Barriers upon barriers have been created.

It is my observation that when people start meditating and they start feeling an upsurge of energy, when they start feeling happy, they immediately come to me and say, "A very strange thing is happening. I am feeling happy, and I am also feeling guilty, for no reason at all." Guilty? They are also puzzled. Why should one feel guilty? They know that they have not done anything wrong. From where does this guilt arise? It is coming from that deep-rooted conditioning that joy is wrong. To be sad is okay, but to be happy is not allowed.

Once I used to live in a town where the police commissioner was my friend; we were friends from the university days. He used to come to me, and he would say, "I am so miserable. Help me to come out of it."

I would say, "You talk about coming out of it, but I don't see that you really want to come out of it. In the first place, why have you chosen to work in this police department? You must be miserable, and you want others also to be miserable."

One day I asked three of my friends to go around the town and dance in different parts of the town and be happy. I said, "You simply go and do this as an experiment." Within one hour, of course, they were caught by the police.

I called the police commissioner; I said, "Why have you caught these friends of mine?"

He said, "These people seem to be mad."

I asked him, "Have they done anything wrong? Have they harmed anybody?"

He said, "No, nothing. Really, they have not done anything wrong."

"Then why have you caught them?"

He said, "But they were dancing in the streets! And they were laughing."

"But if they have not done anything harmful to anybody, why should you interfere? Why should you stop them? They have not attacked anybody, they have not entered anybody's territory. They were just dancing. Innocent people, laughing."

He said, "You are right, but it is dangerous."

"Why is it dangerous? To be happy is dangerous? To be ecstatic is dangerous?" He got the point; he immediately released them. He came running to me; he said, "You may be right. I cannot allow myself to be happy—and I cannot allow anybody else to be happy."

These are your politicians, these are your police commissioners, these are your magistrates, the juries, your leaders, your so-called saints, your priests, your popes—these are the authorities. They all have a great investment in your misery. They depend on your misery. If you are miserable they are happy.

Only a miserable person will go to the temple to pray. A happy person will go to a temple? For what?

I have heard that Adolf Hitler was talking to a British diplomat. They were standing on the thirtieth floor of a skyscraper, and to impress him, he ordered one German soldier to jump off. And the soldier simply jumped without even hesitating, and of course died. The British diplomat could not believe it; it was unbelievable. He was very much shocked. Such a waste? For no reason at all. And to impress him more, Hitler ordered another soldier, "Jump!" and the other jumped. And to impress him even more, he ordered a third soldier.

By this time, the diplomat had come to his senses. He rushed and stopped the soldier and said, "What are you doing, destroying your life for no reason at all?" He said, "Who wants to live, sir, in this country and under this madman? Who wants to live with this Adolf Hitler? It is better to die! It is freedom."

When people are miserable, death seems to be freedom. And when people are miserable, they are so full of rage, anger, that they want to kill—even if the risk is that they may be killed. The politician exists because you are miserable. So Vietnam can continue, Bangladesh, the Arab countries. War continues. Somewhere or other, war continues.

This state of affairs has to be understood—why it exists and how you can drop out of it. Unless you drop out of it, unless you understand the whole mechanism, the conditioning—the hypnosis in which you are living—unless you take hold of it, watch it, and drop it, you will never become ecstatic, and you will never be able to sing the song that you have come to sing. Then you will die without singing your song. Then you will die without dancing your dance. Then you will die without ever having lived.

REAL OR SYMBOLIC?

Your life is just a hope; it is not a reality. It can be a reality.

This neurosis that you call society, civilization, culture, education, this neurosis has a subtle structure. The structure is this: It gives you symbolic ideas so that reality by and by is clouded, becomes clouded, you can't see the real, and you start becoming attached to the unreal. For example, society tells you to be ambitious; it helps you to become ambitious. Ambition means living in hope, living in the tomorrow. Ambition means today has to be sacrificed for tomorrow.

Today is all there is; now is the only time you are, the only time you ever will be. If you want to live, it is now or never.

But society makes you ambitious. From childhood, when you go to school and you are taught ambition, you are poisoned: grow rich, become powerful, become somebody. Nobody tells you that you already have the capacity to be happy. Everybody says that you can have the capacity to be happy only if you fulfill certain conditions—that you have enough money, a big house, a big car, and this and that—only then can you be happy.

Happiness has nothing to do with these things. Happiness is not an achievement, it is your nature. Animals are happy without any money. They are not Rockefellers. And no Rockefeller is as happy as a deer or a dog. Animals have no political power—they are not prime ministers and presidents—but they are happy. The trees are happy; otherwise they would have stopped blooming. They still bloom; the spring still comes. They still dance, they still sing, they still pour their being into the feet of the divine. Their prayer is continuous, their worship never stops. And they don't go to any church; there is no need. God comes to them. In the wind, in the rain, in the sun, God comes to them.

Only man is not happy, because man lives in ambition and not in reality. Ambition is a trick. It is a trick to distract your mind. Symbolic life has been substituted for real life.

Watch it in life. The mother cannot love the child as much as the child wants the mother to love him, because the mother is hung up in her head. Her life has not been one of fulfillment. Her love life has been a disaster. She has not been able to flower. She has lived in ambition. She has tried to control her man, possess him. She has been jealous. She has not been a loving woman. If she has not been a loving woman, how can she suddenly be loving to the child?

I was just reading a book by R. D. Laing. He sent me his book, *The Facts of Life*. In the book he refers to an experiment in which a psychoanalyst asked many mothers, "When your child was going to be born, were you really in a welcoming mood, were you ready to accept the child?" He had made a questionnaire. First question: "Was the child accidental, or did you desire the child?" Ninety percent of the women said, "It was accidental; we did not desire it." Then, "When the pregnancy happened, were you hesitant? Did you want the child, or did you want an abortion? Were you clear about it?" Many of them said that they hesistated for weeks whether to have an abortion or have the child. Then the child was born—they could not decide. Maybe there were other considerations—maybe a religious consideration, it may create sin for them, it may create hell for them. They may have been Catholics, and the idea that abortion is murder prevented them from getting one. Or there might have been social considerations. Or the husband wanted the child, or they wanted to have a child as a continuity of their ego. But the child was not liked. Rarely was there a mother who said, "Yes, the child was welcome. I was waiting for him and I was happy."

Now a child is born who is unwelcome—from the very beginning the mother has been hesitating whether to have it or not to have it. There must be repercussions. The child must feel these tensions. When the mother would think to abort the child, the child must have felt hurt. The child is part of the mother's body; every vibe will reach the child. Or when the mother thinks and hesitates and is just in a limbo of what to do or what not to do, the child will also feel a trembling, shaking—he is hanging between death and life. Then somehow the child is born and the mother thinks it is just accidental—they had tried birth control, they had tried this and that, and everything failed and the child is there—so one has to tolerate it.

That tolerance is not love. The child misses love from the very beginning. And the mother also feels guilty because she is not giving as much love as there would have been naturally. So she starts substituting. She forces the child to eat too much. She cannot fill the child's soul with love; she tries to stuff his body with food. It is a substitute. You can go and see. Mothers are so obsessive. The child says, "I am not hungry," and the mothers go on forcing. They have nothing to do with the child, they don't listen to the child. They are substituting: they cannot give love, so they give food. Then the child grows—they cannot love, so they give money. Money becomes a substitute for love.

And the child also learns that money is more important than love. If you don't have love, nothing to be worried about, but you must have money. In life he will become greedy. He will go after money like a maniac. He will not bother about love. He will say, "First things first. I should first have a big balance in the bank. I must have this much money; only then can I afford love."

Now, love needs no money; you can love as you are. And if you think love needs money and you go after money, one day you may have money and then suddenly you will feel empty—because all the years were wasted in accumulating money. And they are not only wasted; all those years were years of no love, so you have practiced no love. Now the money is there but you don't know how to love. You have forgotten the very language of feeling, the language of love, the language of ecstasy.

Yes, you can purchase a beautiful woman, but that is not love. You can purchase the most beautiful woman in the world, but that is not love. And she will be coming to you not because she loves you; she will be coming to you because of your bank balance.

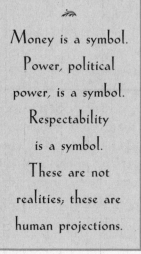

Money is a symbol. Power, political power, is a symbol. Respectability is a symbol. These are not realities; these are human projections.

Money is a symbol. Power, political power, is a symbol. Respectability is a symbol. These are not realities; these are human projections. These are not objectives; they have no objectivity. They are not there, they are just dreams projected by a miserable mind.

If you want to be ecstatic you will have to drop out of the symbolic. To be freed of the symbolic is to be freed of the society. To be freed of the symbolic is to become an individual. To be freed of the symbolic you have taken courage to enter into the real. And only the real is real—the symbolic is not real.

BEING AND BECOMING

What is ecstasy? Something to be achieved? No. Something that you have to earn? No. Something that you have to become? No. Ecstasy is *being* and becoming is misery. If you want to become something you will be miserable. Becoming is the very root cause of misery. If you want to be ecstatic—then it is just now, here and now, this very moment. This very moment—nobody is barring the path—you can be happy. Happiness is so obvious and so easy. It's your nature. You are already carrying it. Just give it a chance to flower, to bloom.

And ecstasy is not of the head, remember. Ecstasy is of the heart. Ecstasy is not of thought; it is of feeling. And you have been deprived of feeling, you have been cut away from feeling. You don't know what feeling is. Even when you say, "I feel," you only think you feel. When you say, "I am feeling happy," watch, analyze, and you will find you *think* you are feeling happy. Even feeling has to pass through thinking. It has to pass through the censor of thinking. Only when thinking approves of it is it allowed. If thinking does not approve of it, it is thrown into the unconscious, into the basement of your being, and forgotten.

Become more of the heart, less of the head. The head is just a part of you; the heart in the sense I am using the word is your whole being. The heart is your totality. So whenever you are total in anything, you function from feeling. Whenever you are partial in anything, you function from the head.

> 🐟
>
> Ecstasy is *being* and becoming is misery. If you want to become something, you will be miserable. If you want to be ecstatic—then it is just now, here and now, this very moment.

Watch a painter painting—and that is the difference between a real artist and a technician. If the painter is just a technician who knows the technique of how to paint, who has the know-how, who knows all about colors and the brushes and the canvas and who has gone through the training, he will function through the head. He will be a technician. He will paint, but he will not be totally in it. Then watch a real artist who is not a technician. He will be absorbed in it, drunk. He will not only paint with his hand, and he will not only paint from his head. He will paint with his whole being; his guts will be involved in it—his feet as well, his blood and bones as well, his marrow, everything will be involved in it. You can watch it, you can see, you can feel he is totally in it, lost. Nothing else exists. He is drunk. In that moment, he is no more.

He is not a doer. The head is a doer. In that moment of total absorption, he is not a doer; he is just a passage, as if the whole is painting through him.

When you come across a dancer—a real dancer, not one who is just a performer—then you will see that he is not dancing, no. Something of the beyond is dancing in him. He is totally in it.

Whenever you are totally into something, you are ecstatic. When you are partially into something, you will remain miserable, because a part will be moving separately from the whole. There will be a division—a split, a tension, anxiety.

If you love from the head, your love is not going to give any ecstatic experience. If you meditate from your head . . .

I used to go to a river to swim, and I loved it. Whenever I came back from swimming, one of my neighbors always used to watch me, and he would see that I was very ecstatic. One day he asked, "What is happening? I always see you going to the river, and for hours you stay there and swim in the river. I am also coming along, because you look so happy."

I said, "Please don't come. You will miss the point, and the river will be very sad. No, don't come, because your very motivation will be a barrier. You can swim, but you will be watching for when that feeling of happiness is going to happen to you. It will never happen—because it happens only when you are *not*."

Swimming can become a meditation, running can become a meditation—anything can become a meditation if you are *not*. Ecstasy is of the heart, is of the total. By *heart* is meant your total, organic unity.

And dance today, not tomorrow. Let the dance be here and now, and let it come from your totality. You abandon yourself; you become a drunkard.

Yes, joy is mad. And only mad people can afford it. The ordinary sane person is so clever, so cunning, calculating, he cannot afford joy, because you cannot control it. Just as I have said that a joyful person cannot be controlled by the society, let me say this also to you: You cannot control your joy, you cannot control your ecstasy. If you want to remain in control, you will never be joyful; then you can only be miserable. Only misery can be controlled—by the society, or even by you.

Many people come to me and they say they would like to get out of their miseries, but they are not ready to move into a state of uncontrol. They want to control joy too. They always want to remain in control. They always want to remain the master, the boss. That is not possible.

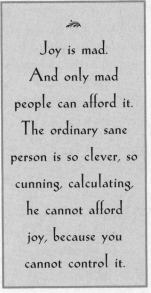

Joy is mad. And only mad people can afford it. The ordinary sane person is so clever, so cunning, calculating, he cannot afford joy, because you cannot control it.

The boss has to go. Joy can erupt in your being only when all control has been removed. Joy knows no control, it is wild.

Ecstasy is wild, you cannot control it. You have to lose all control. You have to drop into it, into the very abyss of it—and it is a bottomless abyss. You go on dropping and dropping and dropping and you never arrive at the bottom because there is no end to joy. It is a nonending process, it is eternal. And it so huge, how can you control it? The very idea is stupid.

When you are madly dancing, madly singing, when you are joyful without any control, without your presence—when the joy is so full, overflowing; you are flooded with it and all control is abandoned—then you will see a miracle. Death and life are dancing together, because then all duality disappears. If *you* are divided, duality appears. If you are undivided, duality disappears.

When you are split, the whole world is split. It is your own split that is projected onto the screen of the universe. When you are in a nonsplit state—integrated, one, organic, orgasmic—then all duality disappears. Then life and death are not two—not opposites, but complementaries dancing with each other hand in hand. Then bad and good are not two—they are dancing with each other hand in hand. Then matter and consciousness are not two. This is what is happening inside you: The soul is dancing with the body; the body is dancing with the soul. They are not two. They are one; they are absolutely one, manifestations of one. The body is nothing but visible soul, and the soul is nothing but invisible body.

And God is not somewhere above in the heavens. He is here now—in the trees, in the rocks, in you, in me, in everything. God is the soul of existence, the invisible, the innermost core. The inner is dancing with the outer. The sublime is dancing with the profane. The holy is dancing with the unholy and the sinner is dancing with the saint.

Once you have become one, suddenly all duality disappears.

That's why I say a really wise man is also a fool, has to be, because foolishness and wisdom dance together. And a really sage person, a real saint, is also a rascal—has to be, it cannot be avoided. God and the devil are not two. Have you ever thought about the word *devil*? It comes from the same root as *divine;* they belong to the same root. They both come from a Sanskrit root, *diva;* from it comes *deva,* from it comes *divine,* from it comes *devil.*

Deep down, the tree is one. Branches are many, moving in

> A really wise man is also a fool, has to be, because foolishness and wisdom dance together. And a really sage person, a real saint, is also a rascal—has to be, it cannot be avoided.

different dimensions, directions; leaves are millions. But the deeper you go, you come to one, one tree.

When you are in a dance, everything dances with you. Yes, the old saying is true: when you weep, you weep alone; when you laugh, the whole world laughs with you. When you are miserable, you are separate.

Misery separates you; separation makes you miserable. They are together, they are one package. Whenever you are miserable you suddenly become separate. That's why the ego cannot afford to be happy, because if you become happy the ego cannot exist—you are no longer separate. The egoist cannot afford to be ecstatic. How can he afford to be ecstatic? Because in ecstasy the ego will not be there. That is too much. He would rather remain miserable. He will create a thousand and one miseries around him just to help the ego to be there.

Have you watched it? When you are really happy, your ego disappears. When you are really happy, suddenly you have a deep feeling of being at one with the whole. When you are miserable you want to be alone; when you are happy you want to share.

When Buddha was miserable he went to the forest, escaped from the world. What happened after six years? When he became ecstatic he came back, back to the marketplace. Whatsoever he has attained has to be shared.

In misery you are like a seed. In ecstasy you become a flower, and your fragrance, of course, has to be released to the winds.

You can watch it in your life also, in a small way. When you are unhappy you close your doors, you don't want to see your friends. You don't want to go anywhere, you don't want to participate in anything. You say, "Leave me alone. Please leave me alone." When somebody becomes very, very unhappy, he commits suicide. What is the meaning of it? What is suicide? Suicide is just an effort to go so far away from the world that one cannot come back. It is moving into loneliness absolutely, irrevocably, so that you cannot come back. That's what suicide is.

Have you ever heard about any man committing suicide when he was happy, when he was ecstatic, when he was dancing? No, when the dance arises, you burst forth, you throw your doors open, you call your friends, you call your neighbors, and you say, "Come. I am going to give a feast—let us dance and let us have a little fun. I have much to share and I would like to give it to you." And whoever comes to your door, you greet them, you welcome them. Everybody is welcome in the moments when you are happy. When you are unhappy, even those who have always been welcome are no longer welcome.

If you dance, the whole of existence becomes a dance. It is already a dance. Hindus say it is a *Ras-Leela*—God is dancing, and around God the stars and the moon and the sun and the earths are dancing around God.

This is the dance that is continuously going on, but you will know it only when you learn the ways of dance, the language of ecstasy.

During the Second World War there was a soldier who would drop his rifle on the battlefield and run to pick up any little scrap of paper, would examine it eagerly, then sorrowfully shake his head as the paper fluttered to the ground. Hospitalized, he remained mute, his compulsion obscure and intractable. He wandered forlornly about the psychiatric ward, picking up scraps of paper, each time with discernible hope followed by inevitable dejection. Pronounced unfit for service, he received one day his discharge from the army, whereupon, receiving the discharge form, he found his voice. "This is it!" he cried in ecstasy. "This is it!"

Ecstasy is the ultimate freedom. And then one simply shouts in joy, "This is it! This is it! Eureka! I have found it."

And the irony is that you need not go anywhere to find it. It is already there. It is your very core, your very being. If you decide to find it, you can find it this very moment. It does not need a single moment's postponement. An intense thirst can open the door. A great urgency can right now make you free.

UNDERSTANDING THE ROOTS OF MISERY

~

RESPONSES TO QUESTIONS

Why don't we drop our miseries, our ignorance and unhappiness? How can human beings be happy and blissful?

Misery has many things to give to you that happiness cannot give. In fact, happiness takes away many things from you. Happiness takes all that you have ever had, all that you have ever been; happiness destroys you. Misery nourishes your ego, and happiness is basically a state of egolessness. That is the problem, the very crux of the problem. That's why people find it very difficult to be happy. That's why millions of people in the world have to live in misery . . . have decided to live in misery. It gives you a very, very crystallized ego. Miserable, you *are*. Happy, you *are not*. In misery there is crystallization; in happiness you become diffused.

If this is understood then things become very clear. Misery makes you special. Happiness is a universal phenomenon, there is nothing special about it. Trees are happy and animals are happy and birds are happy. The whole of existence is happy, except man. Being miserable, man becomes very special, extraordinary.

Misery makes you capable of attracting people's attention.

Whenever you are miserable you are attended to, sympathized with, loved. Everybody starts taking care of you. Who wants to hurt a miserable person? Who is jealous of a miserable person? Who wants to be antagonistic to a miserable person? That would be too mean.

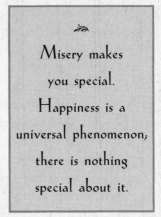

Misery makes you special. Happiness is a universal phenomenon, there is nothing special about it.

The miserable person is cared for, loved, attended to. There is great investment in misery. If the wife is not miserable the husband simply tends to forget her. If she is miserable the husband cannot afford to neglect her. If the husband is miserable the whole family, the wife, the children, are all around him, worried about him; it gives great comfort. One feels one is not alone, one has a family, friends.

When you are ill, depressed, in misery, friends come to visit you, to solace you, to console you. When you are happy, the same friends become jealous of you. When you are really happy, you will find the whole world has turned against you.

Nobody likes a happy person, because the happy person hurts the egos of the others. The others start thinking, "So you have become happy and we are still crawling in darkness, misery, and hell. How dare you be happy when we all are in such misery!"

The world consists of miserable people, and nobody is courageous enough to let the whole world go against him; it is too dangerous, too risky. It is better to cling to misery, it keeps you a part of the crowd. Happy, and you are an individual; miserable, you are part of a crowd—Hindu, Mohammedan, Christian, Indian, Arab, Japanese.

Happy? Do you know what happiness is? Is it Hindu, Christian, Mohammedan? Happiness is simply happiness. One is transported into another world. One is no longer part of the world the human mind has created, one is no longer part of the past, of the ugly history. One is no longer part of time at all. When you are really happy, blissful, time disappears, space disappears.

Albert Einstein has said that in the past scientists used to think that there were two realities—space and time. But he said that these two realities are not two—they are two faces of the same single reality. Hence he coined the word *space-time*, a single word. Time is nothing else but the fourth dimension of space. Einstein was not a mystic, otherwise he would have introduced the third reality also—the transcendental, neither space nor time. That too is there, I call it "the witness." And once these three are there, you have the whole trinity. You have the whole concept of *trimurti*, three faces of God. Then you have all the four dimensions. The reality is four-dimensional: three dimensions of space, and the fourth dimension of time.

But there is something else, which cannot be called the fifth dimension because it is not the fifth really; it is the whole, the transcendental. When you are blissful you start moving into the transcendental. It is not social, it is not traditional, it has nothing to do with human mind at all.

Your question is significant: "What is this attachment to misery?"

There are reasons. Just look into your misery, watch, and you will be able to find what the reasons are. And then look into those moments when once in a while you allow yourself the joy of being in joy, and then see what differences are there.

You will notice a few things: when you are miserable you are a conformist. Society loves it, people respect you, you have great respectability. You can even become a saint; hence your saints are all miserable. The misery is written large on their faces, in their eyes. Because they are miserable they are against all joy. They condemn all joy as hedonism; they condemn every possibility of joy as sin. They are miserable and they would like to see the whole world miserable. In fact only in a miserable world can they be thought to be saints! In a happy world they would have to be hospitalized, mentally treated. They are pathological.

I have seen many saints, and I have been looking into the lives of your past saints. Ninety-nine out of a hundred of them are simply abnormal—neurotic or even psychotic. But they were respected—and they were respected for their misery, remember. The more misery they lived through, the more they were respected. There have been saints who would beat their bodies with a whip every day, and people would gather to see this great austerity, asceticism, penance. The greatest was one who would have wounds all over his body—and these people were thought to be saints! There have been saints who have destroyed their eyes, because it is through the eyes that one becomes aware of beauty, and lust arises. And they were respected because they had destroyed their eyes. They were given eyes to see the beauty of existence, but they decided to become blind. There have been saints who cut off their genital organs, and they were respected very much, tremendously, for the simple reason that they had been self-destructive, violent with themselves. These people were psychologically ill.

Look into your misery and you will find certain fundamental things. It gives you respect. People feel friendlier toward you, more sympathetic. You will have more friends if you are miserable. This is a very strange world, something is fundamentally wrong with it. It should not be so, the happy person should have more friends. But be happy and people become jealous of you, they are no longer friendly. They feel cheated; you have something that is not available to them. Why are you happy? So we have learned down the ages a subtle mechanism to repress happiness and to express misery. It has become second nature.

You have to drop this mechanism. Learn how to be happy, and learn to respect happy people and pay more attention to happy people. This will be a great service to humanity. Don't sympathize too much with people who are miserable. If somebody is miserable, help but don't sympathize. Don't give him the idea that misery is something worthwhile. Let him know perfectly well that you are helping him, but, "this is not out of respect, this is simply because you are miserable." And you are not doing anything but trying to bring the man out of his misery because misery is ugly. Let the person feel that the misery is ugly, that to be miserable is not something virtuous, that he is not doing a great service to humanity.

> Don't sympathize too much with people who are miserable. If somebody is miserable, help but don't sympathize. Don't give him the idea that misery is something worthwhile.

Be happy, respect happiness, and help people to understand that happiness is the goal of life. Whenever you see a blissful person, respect him, he is holy. And wherever you feel a gathering that is blissful, festive, think of it as a sacred place.

We have to learn a totally new language, only then can this old rotten humanity be changed. We have to learn the language of health, wholeness, happiness. It is going to be difficult because our investments are great.

It is one of the most fundamental questions that a person can ask. It is also strange, because it should be easy to drop suffering, anguish, misery. It should not be difficult: You don't want to be miserable, so there must be some deep complication behind it. The complication is that from your very childhood you have not been allowed to be happy, to be blissful, to be joyous.

You have been forced to be serious, and seriousness implies

sadness. You were forced to do things that you never wanted to do. You were helpless, weak, dependent on people; naturally you had to do what they were saying. You did those things unwillingly, miserably, in deep resistance. Against yourself, you have been forced to do so much that by and by one thing became clear to you: that anything that is against you is right, and anything that is not against you is bound to be wrong. And constantly, this whole upbringing filled you with sadness, which is not natural.

To be joyous is natural, just as to be healthy is natural. When you are healthy you don't go to the doctor to inquire, "Why am I healthy?" There is no need for any question about your health. But when you are sick, you immediately ask, "Why am I sick? What is the reason, the cause of my disease?"

It is perfectly all right to ask why you are miserable. It is not right to ask why you are blissful. You have been brought up in an insane society where to be blissful without reason is thought to be madness. If you are simply smiling for no reason at all, people will think something is loose in your head: Why are you smiling? Why are you

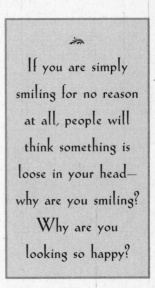

If you are simply smiling for no reason at all, people will think something is loose in your head— why are you smiling? Why are you looking so happy?

looking so happy? And if you say, "I don't know, I am just being happy," your answer will only strengthen their idea that something has gone wrong with you.

But if you are miserable nobody will ask why you are miserable. To be miserable is natural; everybody is. It is nothing special to you. You are not doing something unique.

Unconsciously this idea goes on settling in you, that misery is natural and blissfulness is unnatural. Blissfulness has to be proved. Misery needs no proof. Slowly it sinks deeper into you—into your blood, into your bones, into your marrow—although naturally it is against you. So you have been forced to be a schizophrenic; something that is against your nature has been forced on you. You have been distracted from yourself into something which you are not.

This creates the whole misery of humanity, that everybody is where he should not be, what he should not be. And because he cannot be where he needs to be—where it is his birthright to be—he is miserable. And you have been in this state of going away from yourself farther and farther; you have forgotten the way back home. So wherever you are, you think this is your home—misery has become your home, anguish has become your nature. Suffering has been accepted as health, not as sickness.

And when somebody says, "Drop this miserable life, drop this suffering that you are carrying unnecessarily," a very significant question arises: "This is all that we have got! If we drop it we will be no one, we will lose our identity. At least right now I am somebody—somebody miserable, somebody sad, somebody in suffering. If I drop all this then the question will be, what is my identity? Who am I? I don't know the way back home, and you have taken away the hypocrisy, the false home that was created by the society."

Nobody wants to stand naked in the street.

It is better to be miserable—at least you have something to wear, although it is misery . . . but there is no harm, everybody else is wearing the same kind of clothes. For those who can afford it, their miseries are costly. Those who cannot afford it are doubly miserable—they have to live in a poor kind of misery, nothing much to brag about.

So there are rich miserable people and poor miserable people. And the poor miserable people are trying their hardest to attain somehow the status of rich miserable people. These are the only two types available.

The third type has been completely forgotten. The third is your reality, and it has no misery in it.

You are asking me why man cannot drop his misery; it is for the simple reason that that's all he has got. You want to make him even more poor? He is already poor. There are rich miserable people; he has a small, tiny misery. He cannot brag about it. And you are telling him to drop even this. Then he will be nobody; then he will be empty, a nothingness.

And all the cultures, all the societies, all the religions have committed a crime against humanity: They have created a fear of nothingness, of emptiness.

The truth is that nothingness is the door to richness. Nothingness is the door to blissfulness—and the door has to be nothing. The wall is there; you cannot enter a wall, you will simply hit your head, may have some broken ribs. Why can you not enter the wall? Because the wall has no emptiness, it is solid, it objects. That's why we call things "objects": They are objective, they don't allow you to pass through them, they prevent you.

A door has to be nonobjective, it has to be emptiness. A door means there is nothing to prevent you. You can go in.

And because we have been conditioned that emptiness is something bad, nothingness is something bad, we are being prevented by the conditioning from dropping the misery, dropping the anguish, dropping all the suffering and just being nothing.

The moment you are nothing, you become a door—a door to the divine, a door to yourself, a door that leads to your home, a door that connects you back to your intrinsic nature. And man's intrinsic nature is blissful.

Blissfulness is not something to be achieved.

It is already there; we are born with it.

We have not lost it, we have simply gone farther away, keeping our backs to ourselves.

It is just behind us; a small turn and a great revolution.

And it is not a theoretical question with me. I have just accepted nothingness as a door—which I call meditation, which is nothing but another name for nothingness. And the moment nothingness happens, suddenly you are standing face to face with yourself, and all misery disappears.

The first thing you do is simply to laugh at yourself, at what an idiot you have been. That misery was never there; you were creating it with one hand and you were trying to destroy it with another hand—and naturally you were in a split, in a schizophrenic condition.

It is absolutely easy, simple.

The most simple thing in existence is to be oneself.

It needs no effort; you are already it.

Just a remembrance . . . just getting out of all the stupid ideas that the society has imposed on you. And that is as simple as a snake slipping out of its old skin and never even looking back. It is just an old skin.

If you understand it, it can happen this very moment.

Because this very moment you can see there is no misery, no anguish.

You are silent, standing on the door of nothing; just a step more inward and you have found the greatest treasure that has been waiting for you for thousands of lives.

Why is it so difficult to forgive, to stop clinging to hurts long since past?

The ego subsists on misery—the more misery the more nourishment for it. In blissful moments the ego totally disappears, and vice versa: if the ego disappears, bliss starts showering on you. If you want the ego, you cannot forgive, you cannot forget—particularly the hurts, the wounds, the insults, the humiliations, the nightmares. Not only that you cannot forget, you will go on exaggerating them, you will emphasize them. You will tend to forget all that has been beautiful in your life, you will not remember joyous moments; they serve no purpose as far as the ego is concerned. Joy is like poison to the ego, and misery is like vitamins.

You will have to understand the whole mechanism of the ego. If you try to forgive, that is not real forgiveness. With effort, you will only repress. You can forgive only when you understand the stupidity of the game that goes on within your mind. The total absurdity of it all has to be seen through and through, otherwise you will repress from one side and it will start coming from another side. You will repress in one form; it will assert in another form—sometimes so subtle that it is almost impossible to recognize it, that it is the same old structure, so renovated, refurnished, redecorated, that it looks almost new.

The ego lives on the negative, because the ego is basically a negative phenomenon; it exists on saying no. No is the soul of the ego. And how can you say no to bliss? You can say no to misery, you can say no to the agony of life. How can you say no to the flowers and the stars and the sunsets and all that is beautiful, divine? And the whole of existence is full of it—it is full of roses—but you go on picking the thorns; you have a great investment in those thorns. On the one hand you go on saying, "No, I don't want this misery," and on the other hand you go on clinging to it. And for centuries you have been told to forgive.

But the ego can live through forgiving, it can start having a new nourishment through the idea that, "I have forgiven. I have even forgiven my enemies. I am no ordinary person." And, remember perfectly well, one of the fundamentals of life is that the ordinary person is one who thinks that he is not; the average person is one who thinks that he is not. The moment you accept your ordinariness, you become extraordinary. The moment you accept your ignorance, the first ray of light has entered in your being, the first flower has bloomed. The spring is not far away.

Jesus says: Forgive your enemies, love your enemies. And he is right, because if you can forgive your enemies you will be free of them, otherwise they will go on haunting you. Enmity is a kind of relationship; it goes deeper than your so-called love.

The moment you accept your ordinariness, you become extraordinary. The moment you accept your ignorance, the first ray of light has entered into your being.

Someone asked a question earlier today: "Osho, why does a harmonious love affair seem to be dull and dying?" For the simple reason that it is harmonious! It loses all attraction for the ego; it seems as if it is not. If it is absolutely harmonious you will completely forget about it. Some conflict is needed, some struggle is needed, some violence is needed, some hatred is needed. Love—your so-called love—does not go very deep; it is only skin-deep, or maybe not even so deep. But your hate goes very deep; it goes as deep as your ego.

Jesus is right when he says, "Forgive," but he has been misunderstood for centuries. Buddha says the same thing—all the awakened ones are bound to say the same thing. Their languages can differ, naturally—different ages, different times, different people—they have to speak different languages, but the essential core cannot be different. If you cannot forgive, that means you will live with your enemies, with your hurts, with your pains.

So on the one hand you want to forget and forgive, because the only way to forget is to forgive—if you do not forgive you cannot forget—but on the other hand there is a deeper involvement. Unless you see that involvement, Jesus or Buddha is not going to help. Their beautiful statements will be remembered by you, but they will not become part of your lifestyle, they will not circulate in your blood, in your bones, in your marrow. They will not be part of your spiritual climate; they will remain alien, something imposed from the outside; they are beautiful, intellectually appealing, but existentially you will go on living the same old way.

The first thing to remember is that ego is the most negative phenomenon in existence. It is like darkness. Darkness has no positive existence; it is simply absence of light. Light has a positive existence; that's why you cannot do anything directly with darkness. If your room is full of darkness, you cannot put the darkness out of the room, you cannot throw it out, you cannot destroy it by any means directly. If you try to fight with it, you will be defeated. Darkness cannot be defeated by fighting. You may be a great wrestler but you will be surprised to know that you cannot defeat darkness. It is impossible, for the simple reason that darkness does not exist. If you want to do anything with darkness you will have to go via light. If you don't want darkness, bring light in. If you want darkness, then put the light off. But do something with light; nothing can be done with darkness directly. The negative does not exist—so is the ego.

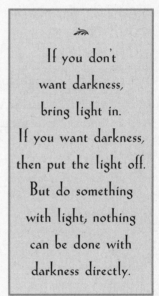

If you don't want darkness, bring light in. If you want darkness, then put the light off. But do something with light, nothing can be done with darkness directly.

That's why I don't suggest that you forgive. I don't say that you should love and not hate. I don't tell you to drop all your sins and

become virtuous. Mankind has tried all that and it has failed completely. My work is totally different. I say: Bring light into your
being. Don't be bothered by all these fragments of darkness.

And at the very center of darkness is ego. Ego is the center of
darkness. You bring light—the method is meditation—you become
more aware, you become more alert. Otherwise you will go on
repressing, and whatsoever is repressed has to be repressed again and
again and again. And it is an exercise in futility, utter futility. It will
start coming up from somewhere else. It will find some other,
weaker point in you.

You ask: "Why is it so difficult to forgive, to stop clinging to
hurts long since past?"

For the simple reason that they are all that you have. And you
go on playing with your old wounds so that they keep fresh in your
memory. You never allow them to heal.

A man was sitting in a compartment in a train. Across from
him was sitting a priest who had a picnic basket beside
him. The man had nothing else to do so he just watched
the priest.

After a while the priest opened the picnic basket and
took out a small cloth, which he placed carefully on his
knees. Then he took out a glass bowl and placed it on the
cloth. Then he took out a knife and an apple, peeled the
apple, cut it up, put the pieces of apple in the bowl. Then
he picked up the bowl, leaned over and tipped the apple
out of the window.

Then he took out a banana, peeled it, cut it up, put it in
the bowl, and tipped it out of the window. The same with a
pear and a little tin of cherries and a pineapple, and a pot of
cream—he tipped them all out of the window after carefully preparing them. Then he cleaned the bowl, dusted off
the cloth, and put them back in the picnic basket.

The man, who had been watching the priest in amazement, finally asked, "Excuse me, Father, but what are you doing there?"

To which the priest replied coolly, "Making fruit salad."

"But you are tipping it all out of the window," said the man.

"Yes," said the priest. "I hate fruit salad."

People go on carrying things that they hate. They live in their hatred. They go on fingering their wounds so they don't heal; they don't allow them to heal—their whole life depends on their past.

Unless you start living in the present, you will not be able to forget and forgive the past. I don't suggest that you should forget and forgive all that has happened in the past; that is not my approach. I say: Live in the present. That is the positive way to approach existence—live in the present. That is another way of saying, Be more meditative, more aware, more alert, because when you are alert, aware, you are in the present.

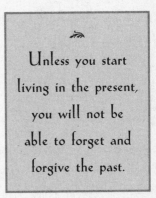

Unless you start living in the present, you will not be able to forget and forgive the past.

Awareness cannot be in the past and cannot be in the future. Awareness knows only the present. Awareness knows no past, no future; it has only one tense, the present. Be aware, and as you start enjoying the present more and more, as you feel the bliss of being in the present, you will stop doing this stupid thing that everybody goes on doing. You will stop going into the past. You will not have to forget and forgive, it will simply disappear of its own accord. You will be surprised—where has it gone? And once the past is there no more, future also disappears because future is only a pro-jection of the past. To be free from past and future is to taste freedom for the first time. And in that experience one be-comes whole, healthy; all wounds are healed. Suddenly there are no longer any wounds; you start feeling a deep well-being arising in you. That well-being is the beginning of transfor-mation.

> To be free from past and future is to taste freedom for the first time. And in that experience one becomes whole, healthy, all wounds are healed.

Why do we make mountains out of molehills?

Because the ego does not feel good, at ease, with molehills—it wants moun-tains. Even if it is misery, it should not be a molehill, it should be an Everest. Even if it is miserable, the ego doesn't want to be ordinar-ily miserable, it wants to be extraordinarily miserable! Either this way or that, one wants to be the first. Hence one goes on making mountains out of molehills.

People go on and on, creating big problems out of nothing. I have talked to thousands of people about their problems and I have not come across a real problem yet! All problems are bogus—you create them, because without problems you feel empty. Without problems, there is nothing to do, nothing to fight with, nowhere to go. People go from one guru to another, from one master to another, from one psychoanalyst to another, from one encounter group to another, because if they don't go they feel empty and they suddenly feel life to be meaningless. You create problems so that you can feel that life is a great work, a growth, and you have to struggle hard.

The ego can exist only when it struggles, remember—when it fights. And the greater the problem, the greater the challenge, the more your ego arises, soars high.

You create problems. Problems don't exist. And now if you allow me, there are not even molehills. That too is your trick. You say, "Okay, there may not be mountains, but there are molehills." No, not even molehills are there—those are your creations. First you create molehills out of nothing, then you create mountains out of molehills.

And the priests and the psychoanalysts and the gurus are happy because their whole trade exists because of you. If you don't create molehills out of nothing, and then if you don't make your molehills into mountains, what will be the point of gurus helping you? First you have to be in a condition to be helped.

> The ego doesn't want to be ordinarily miserable, it wants to be extraordinarily miserable! Either this way or that, one wants to be the first. Hence one goes on making mountains out of molehills.

Please look at what you are doing, what nonsense you are doing. First you create a problem, then you go in search of a solution. Just watch why you are creating the problem. Just exactly in the beginning, when you are creating the problem, is the solution—don't create it! But that won't appeal to you because then you are suddenly thrown flat upon yourself. Nothing to do? No enlightenment, no satori, no samadhi? And you are deeply restless, empty, trying to stuff yourself with anything whatsoever.

You don't have any problems—only this much has to be understood.

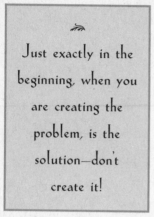

Just exactly in the beginning, when you are creating the problem, is the solution—don't create it!

This very moment you can drop all problems because they are your creations.

So have another look at your problems. The deeper you look, the smaller they will appear. Go on looking at them and by and by they will start disappearing. Go on gazing and suddenly you will find there is emptiness—a beautiful emptiness surrounds you. Nothing to do, nothing to be, because you are already that.

Enlightenment is not something to be achieved, it is just to be lived. When I say I achieved enlightenment, I simply mean that I decided to *live* it. Enough is enough! And since then I have lived it. It is a decision that now you are not interested in creating problems—that's all. It is a decision that now you are finished with all this nonsense of creating problems and finding solutions.

All this nonsense is a game you are playing with yourself. You yourself are hiding and you yourself are seeking—you are both parties. And you know it! That's why when I say it you smile, you laugh. I am not talking about anything ridiculous—you understand it. You are laughing at yourself. Just watch yourself laughing, just look at your own smile—you understand it. It has to be so because it is your own game: You are hiding and waiting for yourself to be able to seek and find yourself.

You can find yourself right now because it is you that is hiding.

That's why Zen masters go on hitting people. Whenever somebody comes and says, "I would like to be a buddha," the master gets very angry. The person is asking nonsense, he *is* a buddha. If Buddha comes to me and asks how to be a buddha, what am I supposed to do? I will hit his head! "Whom do you think you are fooling? You *are* a buddha."

Don't make unnecessary trouble for yourself. And understanding will dawn on you if you watch how you make a problem bigger and bigger and bigger, how you spin it, and how you help the wheel to move faster and faster and faster. Then suddenly you are at the top of your misery and you are in need of the whole world's sympathy.

You are a great problem creator . . . just understand this and suddenly problems disappear. You are perfectly in shape; you are born perfect, that is the whole message. You are born perfect; perfection is your innermost nature. You have just to live it. Decide, and live it.

If you are not yet fed up with the game you can continue, but don't ask why. You know. The why is simple. The ego cannot exist in emptiness, it needs something to fight with. Even a ghost of your imagination will do, but you need to fight with someone. The ego exists only in conflict—the ego is not an entity, it is a tension. Whenever there is a conflict, the tension arises and the ego exists; when there is no conflict, the tension disappears and the ego disappears. Ego is not a thing, it is just a tension.

And of course nobody wants small tensions, everybody wants big tensions. If your own problems are not enough, you start thinking about humanity and the world and the future . . . socialism, communism, and all that rubbish. You start thinking about it as if the whole world depends on your advice. Then you think, "What is going to happen in Israel? What is going to happen in Africa?" And you go on advising, and you create problems.

People become very excited, they cannot sleep because there is some war going on. They become very excited. Their own life is so ordinary that they will have to get extraordinariness from some other source. The nation is in difficulty so they become identified with the nation. The culture is in difficulty, the society is in difficulty—now there are big problems and you become identified. You are a Hindu and the Hindu culture is in difficulty; you are a Christian and the church is in difficulty. The whole world is at stake. Now you become big through your problem.

The ego needs some problems. If you understand this, in the very understanding the mountains become molehills again, and then the molehills also disappear. Suddenly there is emptiness, pure emptiness all around. This is what enlightenment is all about—a deep understanding that there is no problem.

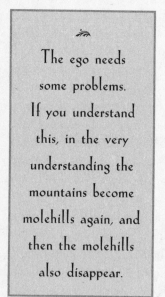

The ego needs some problems. If you understand this, in the very understanding the mountains become molehills again, and then the molehills also disappear.

Then, with no problem to solve, what will you do? Immediately you start living. You will eat, you will sleep, you will love, you will have a chitchat, you will sing, you will dance—what else is there to do? You have become a god, you have started living.

If there is any God, one thing is certain: He will not have any problems. That much is certain. Then what is he doing with all his time? No problems, no psychiatrist to consult, no gurus to go and surrender to . . . what is God doing? What will he do? He must be going crazy, spinning! No—he is living; his life is totally full with life. He is eating, sleeping, dancing, having a love affair—but without any problems.

Start living this very moment and you will see that the more you live, the fewer problems there are. Because now that your emptiness is flowering and living, there is no need. When you don't live, the same energy goes sour. The same energy that would have become a flower is stuck. And not being allowed to bloom, it becomes a thorn in the heart. It is the same energy.

Force a small child to sit in the corner and tell him to become completely immobile, unmoving. Watch what happens . . . just a few minutes before, he was perfectly at ease, flowing; now his face will become red because he will have to strain, hold himself. His whole body will become rigid and he will try to fidget here and there and he will want to jump out of himself. You have forced the energy to sit still—now it has no purpose, no meaning, no space to move, nowhere to bloom and flower; it is stuck, frozen, rigid. The child is suffering a death, a temporary death. Now if you don't allow the child to run again and move around the garden and play, he will start creating problems. He will fantasize; in his mind he will create problems and start fighting with those problems. He will see a big dog and he will be afraid, or he will see a ghost and he will have to fight and escape from him. Now he is creating problems—the same energy that was just flowing all around a moment before, in all directions, is stuck and becoming sour.

> If people can dance a little more, sing a little more, be a little crazier, their energy will be flowing more and their problems will by and by disappear.

If people can dance a little more, sing a little more, be a little crazier, their energy will be flowing more and their problems will by and by disappear.

Hence I insist so much on dance. Dance to orgasm; let the whole energy become dance, and suddenly you will see that you don't have any head—the energy stuck in the head is moving all around, creating beautiful patterns, pictures, movement. And when you dance there comes a moment when your body is no longer a rigid thing, it becomes flexible, flowing. When you dance there comes a moment when your boundary is no longer so clear; you melt and merge with the cosmos, the boundaries are mixing.

Watch a dancer—you will see that he has become an energy phenomenon, no longer in a fixed form, no longer in a frame. He is flowing out of his frame, out of his form, and becoming more alive, more and more alive. But only if you dance yourself will you know what really happens. The head inside disappears; again you are a child. Then you don't create any problems.

Live, dance, eat, sleep, do things as totally as possible. And remember again and again: Whenever you catch yourself creating any problem, slip out of it, immediately. Once you get *into* the problem then a solution will be needed. And even if you find a solution, out of that solution a thousand and one problems will arise again. Once you miss the first step you are in the trap.

Whenever you see that now you are slipping into a problem, catch hold of yourself—run, jump, dance, but don't get into the problem. Do something immediately so that the energy that was creating the problems becomes fluid, unfrozen, melts, goes back to the cosmos.

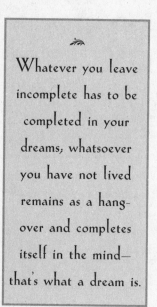

Whatever you leave incomplete has to be completed in your dreams; whatsoever you have not lived remains as a hangover and completes itself in the mind— that's what a dream is.

Primitive people don't have many problems. I have come across primitive groups in India who say they don't dream at all. Freud would not be able to believe that it is possible. They don't dream, but if sometimes somebody dreams—it is a rare phenomenon—the whole village fasts, prays to God. Something has gone wrong, something wrong has happened . . . a man has dreamed. It never happens in their tribe because they live so totally that nothing is left in the head to be completed in sleep.

Whatever you leave incomplete has to be completed in your dreams; whatsoever you have not lived remains as a hang-over and completes itself in the mind—that's what a dream is. The whole day you go on thinking. The thinking simply shows that you have more energy than you use for living; you have more energy than your so-called life needs.

You are missing real life. Use more energy, then fresh energies will be flowing. Just don't be a miser. Use them today; let today be complete; tomorrow will take care of itself, don't be worried about tomorrow. The worry, the problem, the anxiety, all simply show one thing: that you are not living rightly, that your life is not yet a celebration, a dance, a festivity. Hence all the problems.

If you live, ego disappears. Life knows no ego, it knows only living and living and living. Life knows no self, no center; life knows no separation. You breathe—life enters into you. You exhale—you enter into life. There is no separation. You eat, and trees enter into you through the fruit. Then one day you die, you are buried in the earth, and the trees suck you up and you become fruits. Your children will eat you again. You have been eating your ancestors; the trees have converted them into fruits. You think you are a vegetarian? Don't be deceived by appearances. We are all cannibals.

Life is one, it goes on moving. It comes into you; it passes through you. In fact, to say that it comes into you isn't right, because then it seems as if life comes into you, and then passes out of you. You don't exist—only this life's coming and going exists. You don't exist—only life exists in its tremendous forms, in its energy, in its millions of delights. Once you understand this, let that understanding be the only law.

Why do I always feel so miserable? Can't you take it all away?

The answer is in your question. You don't want to take responsibility for your own being, somebody else should do it. And that's the sole cause of misery.

There is no way that anybody else can take away your misery.

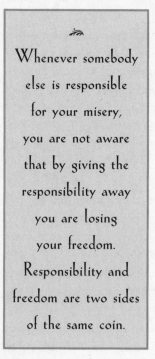

Whenever somebody else is responsible for your misery, you are not aware that by giving the responsibility away you are losing your freedom. Responsibility and freedom are two sides of the same coin.

There is no way that anybody else can make you blissful. But if you become aware that you are responsible for whether you are miserable or blissful, that nobody else can do anything . . .

Your misery is your doing; your bliss will also be your doing.

But it is hard to accept—misery is my doing?

Everyone feels that others are responsible for their misery. The husband thinks the wife is responsible for their misery, the wife thinks the husband is responsible for her misery, the children think the parents are responsible for their misery, the parents think the children are responsible for their misery. It has become such a complexity. And whenever somebody else is responsible for your misery, you are not aware that by giving the responsibility away, you are losing your freedom. Responsibility and freedom are two sides of the same coin.

And because you think others are responsible for your misery, that's why there are charlatans, so-called saviors, messengers of God, prophets who go on telling you, "You have not to do anything, just follow me. Believe in me and I will save you. I am your shepherd, you are my sheep."

Strange that not a single person stood up against people like Jesus Christ and said, "It is utterly insulting to say that you are the shepherd and we are sheep, that you are the savior and we are just dependent on your compassion, that our whole religion is just to believe in you." But because we have been throwing the responsibility for our misery on others, we have accepted the corollary that bliss will also come from others.

Naturally, if misery comes from others, then bliss has to come from others. But then what are *you* doing? You are neither responsible for misery nor are you responsible for bliss—then what is your function? What is your purpose?—just to be a target for a few people to make you miserable and for others to help you and save you and make you blissful? Are you just a puppet, and all the strings are in the hands of others?

You are not respectful of your humanity; you do not respect yourself. You don't have any love for your own being, for your own freedom.

If you are respectful of your life, you will refuse all the saviors. You will say to all the saviors, "Get lost! Just save yourself, that's enough. It is my life and I have to live it. If I do something wrong, I will suffer the misery; I will accept the consequences of my wrong action without any complaint."

Perhaps that is the way one learns—by falling, one gets up again; by going astray, one comes back again. You commit a mistake . . . but each mistake makes you more intelligent; you will not commit the same mistake again. If you commit the same mistake again, that means you are not learning. You are not using your intelligence, you are behaving like a robot.

My whole effort is to give back to every human being the self-respect that belongs to him—which he has given to just anybody.

And the whole stupidity starts because you are not ready to accept that for your misery, you are responsible.

Just think: You cannot find a single misery for which you are not responsible. It may be jealousy, it may be anger, it may be greed—but something in you must be creating the misery.

And have you ever seen anybody in the world making anybody else blissful? That too depends on you, on your silence, your love, your peace, your trust. And the miracle happens—nobody does it.

In Tibet, there is a beautiful story about Marpa. It may not be factual, but it is tremendously significant. I don't care much about facts. My emphasis is on the significance and the truth, which is a totally different thing.

Marpa heard about a master. He was searching and he went to the master, he surrendered to the master, he trusted totally. And he asked the master, "What am I supposed to do now?"

The master said, "Once you have surrendered to me, you are not supposed to do anything. Just believe in me. My name is the only secret mantra for you. Whenever you are in difficulty, just remember my name and everything will be all right."

Marpa touched his feet. And he tried it immediately, he was such a simple man—he walked on the river. Other disciples who had been with the master for years could not believe it—he was walking on the water! They reported to the master, "That man, you have not understood him. He is no ordinary man, he is walking on water!"

The master said, "What?"

They all ran toward the river and Marpa was walking on the water, singing songs, dancing. When he came to the shore, the master asked, "What is the secret?"

He said, "What is the secret? It is the same secret you have given to me—your name. I remembered you. I said, 'Master, allow me to walk on water,' and it happened."

The master could not believe that his name could do this. He himself could not walk on water. But who knows . . . he had never tried. He thought it would be better to check a few more things before he tried, though, so he said to Marpa, "Can you jump from that cliff?"

Marpa said, "Whatever you say." He went up on the hill and jumped from the cliff, and they were all standing in the valley waiting—just pieces of Marpa will be left! Even if they could find pieces of him, that would be enough of a miracle—the hill was very high.

But Marpa came down smiling, sitting in a lotus posture. He landed just under a tree in the valley, and sat down. They all surrounded him. They looked at him—not even a scratch.

The master said, "This is something! You used my name?"

He said, "It was your name."

The master said, "This is enough, now I am going to try," and with the first step in the water, he sank.

Marpa could not believe it when the master sank. His disciples jumped in and somehow pulled him out; he was half dead. The water was taken out of his lungs . . . somehow he survived.

Marpa said, "What is the matter?"

The master said, "You must forgive me. I am no master, I am just a pretender."

But Marpa said, "If you are a pretender, then how did your name work?"

The pretender said, "My name has not worked, it is your trust. It does not matter who you trust—it is the trust, the love, the totality of it. I don't trust myself. I don't trust anybody. I cheat everybody—how can I trust? And I am always afraid to be cheated by others, because I am cheating. Trust is impossible for me. You are an innocent man, you trusted me. It is because of your trust that the miracles have happened."

Whether the story is true or not does not matter.

One thing is certain, that your misery is caused by your mistakes and your bliss is caused by your trust, by your love.

Your bondage is your creation and your freedom is your declaration.

You are asking me, "Why am I miserable?" You are miserable because you have not accepted the responsibility for it. Just see what your misery is, find out the cause—and you will find the cause within yourself. Remove the cause and the misery will disappear.

But people don't want to remove the cause, they want to remove the misery. That is impossible, that is absolutely unscientific.

And then you ask me to save you, to help you. There is no need for you to become a beggar. You are not to become beggars. You are not sheep, you are emperors.

Accept your responsibility for misery and you will find that hidden inside you are all the causes of bliss, freedom, joy, enlightenment, immortality. No savior is needed. And there has never been any savior; all saviors are pseudo. They have been worshiped because you always wanted somebody to save you. They have always appeared because they were always in demand, and wherever there is a demand, there is a supply.

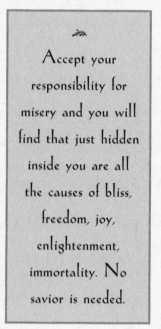

Accept your responsibility for misery and you will find that just hidden inside you are all the causes of bliss, freedom, joy, enlightenment, immortality. No savior is needed.

Once you depend on others, you are losing your soul. You are forgetting that you have a consciousness as universal as anybody else's, that you have a consciousness as great as any Gautam Buddha's—you are just not aware of it, you have not looked for it. And you have not looked because you are looking at others—somebody else to save you, somebody else to help you. You go on begging without recognizing that this whole kingdom is yours.

This has to be understood as one of the most basic principles— of self-respect and freedom and responsibility.

Why does everyone want to pretend to be what they are not? What is the psychology behind it?

It is because everybody is condemned from his very childhood. Whatever he does on his own, of his own accord, is not acceptable. The people, the crowd in which a child has to grow up, have their own ideas and ideals. The child has to fit with those ideas and ideals. The child is helpless.

Have you ever thought about it? The human child is the most helpless child in the whole animal kingdom. All the animals can survive without the support of the parents and the crowd, but the human child cannot survive, he will die immediately. He is the most helpless creature in the world—so vulnerable to death, so delicate. Naturally those who are in power are able to mold the child in the way they want.

So everybody has become what he is, against himself. That is the psychology behind the fact that everybody wants to pretend to be what he is not.

Everybody is in a schizophrenic state. They have never been allowed to be themselves, they have been forced to be somebody else that their nature does not allow them to be happy with.

So as one grows and stands on his own legs, one starts pretending many things, which one would have liked in reality to be part of one's being. But in this insane world, everybody has been distracted. Each person has been made into somebody else; they are not that, and they know it. Everybody knows that they have been forced—to become a doctor, to become an engineer, to become a politician, to become a criminal, to become a beggar. There are all kinds of forces around.

In Bombay in India there are people whose sole business is to steal children and make them crippled, blind, lame, and force them to beg and to bring back all the money that they have gathered each evening. Yes, food will be given to them, shelter will be given to them. They are being used as commodities, they are not human beings. This is the extreme, but the same has happened with everybody to a lesser or greater extent. Nobody is at ease with himself.

In this world, there is only one happiness and that is to be yourself. And because nobody is himself, everybody is trying somehow to hide—with masks, pretensions, hypocrisies. They are ashamed of what they are.

> 🐦
> Everybody is trying somehow to hide—with masks, pretensions, hypocrisies. They are ashamed of what they are.

We have made the world a marketplace, not a beautiful garden where everybody is allowed to bring his own flowers. We are forcing marigolds to bring forth roses—now from where can marigolds produce roses? Those roses will be plastic roses, and in its heart of hearts the marigold will be crying, and feeling ashamed that "I have not been courageous enough to rebel against the crowd. They have forced plastic flowers on me, and I have my own real flowers for which my juices are flowing—but I cannot show my real flowers."

You are being taught everything, but you are not being taught to be yourself. This is the ugliest form of society possible, because it makes everybody miserable.

To be what you don't want to be, to be with someone you don't want to be with, to do something you don't want to do, these things are the basis of all your miseries.

And on the one hand the society has managed to make

everybody miserable, and on the other hand the same society expects that you should not show your misery—at least not in public, not in the open. It is your private business.

They have created it—it really is public business, not private business. The same crowd that has created all the reasons for your misery finally says to you: "Your misery is your own, but when you come out, come out smiling. Don't show your miserable face to others." This they call etiquette, manners, culture. Basically, it is hypocrisy.

Sooner or later you have to decide. You have to say, "Whatever the cost, I want just to be myself. Condemned, unaccepted, losing respectability—everything is okay but I cannot pretend anymore to be somebody else." This decision and this declaration—this declaration of freedom, freedom from the weight of the crowd—gives birth to your natural being, to your individuality.

Then you don't need any mask. Then you can be simply yourself, just as you are.

How can I be myself?

That should be the easiest thing in the world, but it is not. To be oneself one need not do anything; one already is. How can you be otherwise? How can you be anybody else? But I can understand the problem. The problem arises because the society corrupts everybody. It corrupts the mind, the being. It enforces things on you and you lose contact with yourself. It tries to make something else out of you than that which you were meant to be. It puts you off your center. It drags you away from yourself. It teaches you to be like a Christ or to be like a Buddha or to be like this and that; it never says to you to be yourself. It never allows you freedom to be; it enforces foreign, outside images on your mind.

Then the problem arises. You can pretend, but when you pretend you are never satisfied. You always want to be yourself—that is natural—and the society does not allow it. It wants you to be somebody else. It wants you to be phony. It does not want you to be real, because real people are dangerous people; real people are rebellious. Real people cannot be controlled so easily, they cannot be regimented. Real people will live their reality in their own way—they will do their thing; they won't bother about other things. You cannot sacrifice them in the name of religion, in the name of the state, nation, race. It is impossible to seduce them for any sacrifice. Real people are always for their own happiness. Their happiness is ultimate: They are not ready to sacrifice it for anything else. That's the problem.

So the society distracts every child: It teaches the child to be somebody else. And by and by the child learns the ways of pretension, hypocrisy. And one day—this is the irony—the same society starts talking to you in this way, starts saying to you: What has happened to you? Why are you not happy? Why do you look miserable? Why are you sad? And then come the priests. First they corrupt you, they distract you from the path of happiness—because there is only one happiness possible and that is to be yourself—then they come and say to you: Why are you unhappy? Why are you miserable? And then they teach you ways to be happy. First they make you ill, and then they sell medicines. It is a great conspiracy.

I have heard . . .

A little old Jewish lady sits down on a plane next to a big Norwegian. She keeps staring and staring at him. Finally she turns to him and says, "Pardon me, are you Jewish?"

He replies, "No."

A few minutes go by, and she looks at him again and asks, "You can tell me—you are Jewish, aren't you?"

He answers, "Definitely not."

She keeps studying him and says again, "I can tell you are Jewish."

In order to get her to stop annoying him the gentleman replies, "Okay, I'm Jewish."

She looks at him and shakes her head back and forth, and says, "You don't look it."

That's how things are. You ask, "How can I be myself?" Just drop the pretensions, just drop this urge to be somebody else, just drop this desire to look like Christ, Buddha, to look like your neighbor. Drop competition and drop comparison and you will be yourself. Comparison is the poison. You are always thinking in terms of how the other is doing. He has a big house and a big car and you are miserable. He has a beautiful woman and you are miserable. He is climbing up the staircase of power and politics and you are miserable. Compare, and you will imitate. If you compare yourself with rich people, you will start running in the same direction. If you compare yourself with learned people, you will start accumulating knowledge. If you compare yourself with the so-called saints, you will start accumulating virtue—and you will be imitative. And to be imitative is to miss the whole opportunity to be oneself.

Drop comparison. You are unique. Nobody else is like you, nobody else has ever been like you, and nobody else is ever going to be like you. You are simply unique—and when I am saying you are unique, I am not saying you are better than others, remember. I am simply saying they are also unique. To be unique is an ordinary quality of every being. To be unique is not a comparison, to be unique is as natural as breathing.

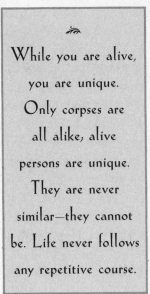

While you are alive, you are unique. Only corpses are all alike, alive persons are unique. They are never similar—they cannot be. Life never follows any repetitive course.

Everybody is breathing and everybody is unique. While you are alive, you are unique. Only corpses are all alike; living persons are unique. They are never similar—they cannot be. Life never follows any repetitive course. Existence never repeats: It goes on singing a new song every day, paints something new every day.

Respect your uniqueness, and drop comparison. Comparison is the culprit. Once you compare, you are on the track. Don't compare with anybody—the other person is not you, you are not the other person. Let others be, and you relax into your being. Start enjoying whatsoever you are. Delight in the moments that are available to you.

Comparison brings in the future, comparison brings ambition, and comparison brings violence. You start fighting, struggling, you become hostile.

Life is not something like a commodity. Happiness is not something like a commodity such that if others have it, you cannot—"If others have happiness how can I have it?"—happiness is not a commodity at all. You can have as much as you want. It simply depends on you. Nobody is competitive about it, nobody is a competitor to you. Just as the garden is beautiful—you can look and appreciate it, somebody else can look and appreciate it. Because somebody else is appreciating the garden and saying it is beautiful, you are not hindered; the other is not exploiting you. The garden is not less because another person has appreciated it; because someone else is enthralled by its beauty, the garden is not less. In fact, the garden is more beautiful; because someone has appreciated it, that person has added a new dimension to the garden.

People who are happy are in fact adding some quality to existence—just by being happy they are creating vibes of happiness. You can appreciate this world more and more if more and more people are happy. Don't think in terms of competition. It is not that if they are happy, how can you be happy, so you have to jump on them and snatch happiness away, you have to compete.

Remember, if people are unhappy it will be very difficult for you to be happy. Happiness is available to everybody—for whoever opens his heart, happiness is always available.

It is not that somebody has achieved something. It is not like a political post—one person has become the president of a country, now everybody cannot become the president, true. But if one person has become enlightened, that does not hinder anybody else from becoming enlightened—in fact, it helps. Because Buddha became enlightened it has become easier for you to become enlightened. Because Christ became enlightened it has become easier for you. Somebody has walked on the path; the footprints are there, that person has left subtle hints for you. You can go more easily, in deeper confidence, with less hesitation. The whole earth can become enlightened—each single being can become enlightened. But everybody cannot become a president.

A given country has hundreds of millions of people—only one person can become the president; of course it is a competitive thing. But hundreds of millions of people can become enlightened, that's not a problem.

All that is transcendent is noncompetitive—and your being is transcendent. So just sort it out. Society has muddled your head; it has taught you the competitive way of life. Meditation is a noncompetitive way of life. Society is ambition; meditativeness, awareness, is nonambitious. And when you are nonambitious, only then can you be yourself. This is simple.

Sometimes I feel, not like Sartre says, that "hell is other people," but that "hell is myself." I am in hell. Hell! Do I have to accept hell before I can find bliss? I don't understand how.

No, you are not in hell. You *are* hell. The very ego is hell. Once the ego is not there, there is no hell. The ego creates structures around you, which make you miserable. The ego functions like a wound—then everything starts hurting it. The *I* is hell.

Self is hell, no-self is heaven. Not to be, is to be in heaven. To be is always to be in hell. "Do I have to accept hell before I can find bliss?" You have to *understand* hell, because if you don't understand hell, you will never be able to get out of it. And for understanding, acceptance is a must. You cannot understand anything if you go on denying it. That's what we have been doing. We go on disowning parts of our being. We go on insisting, "This is not me." Jean-Paul Sartre says the other is hell—when you deny something in yourself, you project it on the other.

Look at the mechanism of projection. Whatever you deny in yourself, you project on others. You have to put it somewhere. It is there, you know.

Just the other night a woman told me that she has become very afraid that her husband is going to kill her. Now, she has a very simple and beautiful husband, a very simple man. Rarely can you find such simple people. It is almost absurd, the idea that he is going to kill her. When she was saying it, the husband started crying. The very idea was so absurd, tears started falling from his eyes. It is very rare to see a man crying, because men have been trained not to cry. He felt it—what to do? And the woman thinks that any moment the husband is going to suffocate her. She feels his hands on her neck in the darkness. Now, what is happening?

Then by and by she talked about other things. She has no child, and she desperately wants a child. She told me that looking at others' children she feels that she would like to kill them. Now things are clear. Now nothing is complicated. She said she would like to kill the others' children because she has no child and she would not like anybody else to be a mother. Now this murderer is in her, and she does not want to accept it. It has to be projected on somebody else. She cannot accept that she has a murderous instinct; it has to be projected. It is very difficult to accept that you are a murderer, or that you have ideas of murdering children.

Now, the husband is the closest person, the one most available to be projected on, almost like a screen. Now the poor man is crying and the woman thinks he is going to murder her. In the deep unconscious she may even have ideas of murdering the husband, because she must have a certain logic inside—because of this man she is not getting pregnant. If she were with some other man, she would have become a mother. She would not accept it on the surface, but deep down she must be feeling that because of this man being her husband, she has not been able to become a mother. Somewhere in the unconscious there is the shadow of a thought lurking, that if this man dies, she will be able to find another man—or something like that. And then the idea that she would like to kill others' children . . . She is projecting it. And when you project your ideas on others, you become frightened of them. Now this man looks like a murderer to her.

We all do this. If you deny some part of your being, if you disown it, where will you put it? You will have to put it on somebody else.

Wars have continued, conflicts will continue, violence will continue unless man comes to understand not to deny anything in himself but to accept it. Reabsorb it into your organic unity, because the denied part will create many troubles for you. Whatsoever you deny, you will have to put somewhere else. You will have to project it onto somebody. The denied part becomes a projection, and the eyes that project live in illusion. Then they are not realistic.

Jean-Paul Sartre says, "Hell is other people." This is something to be understood. You always think in that way. He is simply expressing a very common misunderstanding, a very common illusion. If you are miserable you think somebody else is making you miserable. If you are angry you think somebody is making you angry—but always somebody else.

If you are angry, *you* are angry. If you are miserable, *you* are miserable. Nobody is making you that way. Nobody can make you angry unless you decide to become angry. Then everybody can be a help, then everybody can be used as a screen and you can project. Nobody can make you miserable unless you decide to be miserable. Then the whole world helps you to be miserable.

The self is hell, not the other. The very idea that "I am separate from the world" is hell. Separation is hell. Drop the ego and see suddenly—all misery disappears, all conflict disappears.

You ask, "Do I have to accept hell before I can find bliss?" Certainly, absolutely. You will have to accept and understand. In that acceptance and understanding, the hell will be absorbed back into the unity. Your conflict will dissolve, your tension will dissolve. You will become more of one piece, you will be more together. And when you are together, there is no idea of ego at all.

Ego is a disease. When you are pulled apart, when you live in a split way, moving in many dimensions and directions that are simultaneously against each other, when you live in contradiction, then the ego arises.

Have you ever felt your head without a headache? When the headache is there you feel the head. If all headache disappears, the head disappears; you will never feel it is there. When you are ill you feel the body; when you are healthy you don't feel it. Perfect health is bodilessness; you don't feel the body at all. You can forget the body; there is nothing pulling you to remember it. A perfectly healthy person is one who is oblivious of the body; he does not remember that he has a body.

A child is perfectly healthy; he has no body. The old man has a big body; the older one becomes, the more illness, disease, conflict settles in. Then the body is not functioning as it should function, is not in harmony, is not in accord. Then one feels the body more.

If you understand this simple phenomenon, that a headache makes you aware of the head, illness makes you aware of the body, then it must be something like an illness in your soul that makes you aware of the self. Otherwise a perfectly healthy soul will not have any self. That's what Gautam Buddha says—there is no self. Only no-self exists, and that is the heavenly state. You are so healthy and so harmonious that there is no need to remember the self.

But ordinarily we go on cultivating the ego. On one hand we go on trying not to be miserable and on the other hand we go on cultivating the ego. All our approaches are contradictory.

I have heard:

A haughty socialite died and arrived at the gates of heaven. "Welcome, come right in," was Saint Peter's greeting.

"I will not," she sneered. "If you just let anyone in without a reservation, this is not my idea of heaven."

If the egoist, even by chance, reaches the gates of heaven, he will not enter. This is not his idea of heaven—without a reservation anybody is welcome? Then what is the point? Only very few chosen persons, rare persons, should be allowed. Then the ego can enter heaven. In fact the ego cannot enter heaven, it can only enter hell. It will be better to say the ego carries its own hell wherever it goes.

It happened:

Mulla Nasruddin fell into a cesspool in the countryside and was not able to work his way out. So he stood there yelling, "Fire! Fire!" and in a couple of hours the firemen finally arrived.

"There is no fire here!" exclaimed the chief. "What are you yelling 'Fire' for?"

"What did you want me to yell?" demanded the Mulla. " 'Shit'?"

The ego is such that even if it is in hell, it will not admit it. The ego goes on decorating itself.

You ask, "Do I have to accept hell before I can find bliss?"

There is no other way. You will not only have to accept, you will have to understand and penetrate. You will have to suffer the pangs and the pain of it so that you become perfectly aware what it is. Only when you know what it is will you be able to know how you create it. And only when you know how you create it, then it is up to you whether you want to create it any more or not. Then it is your choice. "I don't understand how," you say. Yes, it is difficult to accept hell. Our whole effort is to deny it. That's why you may be crying within but you go on smiling on the outside. You may be sad but you go on pretending you are happy. It is hard to accept that you are miserable. But if you go on denying it, it will by and by become disconnected from your awareness.

That's what happens when we say something has become unconscious. It means it has become disconnected from consciousness. You have denied it so long that it has receded into the shadow part of your life, it has moved into the basement. You never come across it, but it goes on working from there and affecting you and poisoning your being.

If you are miserable you can smile, but that smile is painted on. It is just an exercise of the lips. It has nothing to do with your being. You can smile, you can persuade a woman to fall in love with your smile. But remember—she is doing the same. She is also smiling and miserable. She is also pretending. So two false smiles create the situation we call "love." But how long can you go on smiling? You will have to relax. After a few hours you will have to relax.

If you have a penetrating eye, you can see—if you live with a person for three hours you can see his reality. Because to pretend for even three hours is very difficult. How to go on smiling for three hours if there is no smile coming from you? You will forget again and again and your miserable face will show.

For a few moments you can deceive. That's how we deceive each other. And we promise that we are very happy persons, but we are not. The same is done by the other. Then every love affair becomes a misery, and every friendship.

By hiding your misery you are not going to get out of it—you will create more misery. The first thing is to encounter it. Never move unless you have encountered your reality, and never pretend to be somebody else. That is not the way happiness ever happens.

Just be yourself. If you are miserable, then be miserable. Nothing wrong is going to happen. You will be saved many troubles. Of course nobody will fall in love with you; okay—you will be saved many troubles. You will remain alone, but nothing is wrong in being alone. Face it, go deep into it, take it out, uproot it from the unconscious and bring it to the conscious. It is hard work, but the payoff is immense. Once you have seen it, you can simply throw it away. It exists unseen, it exists only in the unconscious, in the darkness. Once you bring it to light, it starts withering.

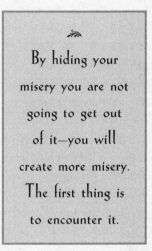

By hiding your misery you are not going to get out of it—you will create more misery. The first thing is to encounter it.

Bring your whole mind to light and you will see—all that is miserable starts dying and all that is beautiful and blissful starts sprouting. In the light of consciousness, that which remains is good, and that which dies is bad. That's my definition of sin and virtue. Sin is that which cannot grow with awareness; it needs unawareness to grow. Unawareness is a must for it. Virtue is that which can grow with absolute awareness; there is no difficulty.

Whenever in life I've had a bout of feeling miserable because of the end of a relationship, a point always comes when I just laugh at myself, feel freedom return, and see that all I had done was to stop loving myself. Is this at the root of most people's suffering, or is it just my trip?

It is not just your trip. It is at the root of most people's suffering—but not with the meaning you are giving to it. It is not because you have stopped loving yourself that you fall into misery. It is that you have created a self that does not exist at all. So sometimes this unreal self suffers misery in loving others, because love is not possible when it is based in unreality. And it is not just on one side: two unrealities trying to love each other . . . sooner or later this arrangement is going to fail. When this arrangement fails, you fall back upon yourself—there is nowhere else to go. So you think, "I had forgotten to love myself."

In a way it is a small relief, at least instead of two unrealities now you have only one. But what will you accomplish by loving yourself? And how long can you manage to keep loving yourself? It is unreal; it won't allow you to look at it for a long time because that is dangerous: If you look into it for a long time, this so-called self will disappear. That will be a *real* freedom from misery. Love will remain—neither addressed to someone else nor to yourself. Love will be unaddressed because there is nobody to address, and when love is there, unaddressed, there is great bliss.

But this unreal self won't allow you much time for that. Soon you will be falling in love with someone else again, because the unreal self needs the support of other unrealities. So people fall in love and fall out of love and fall in love and fall out of love—and it is a strange phenomenon that they do it dozens of times and still they don't see the point. They are miserable when they are in love with someone else; they are miserable when they are alone and not in love, although a bit relieved—for the moment.

In India, when a person dies, people place the body on a stretcher and carry it on their shoulders to the funeral pyre. But they go on changing the position of it along the way—from the left shoulder they will put the weight of the stretcher on the right, and after a few minutes they will again change and put it on the left. It feels like a relief when you shift it from the left shoulder onto the right. Nothing is being changed—the weight is still there, and it is resting on you, but the left shoulder feels a kind of relief. It is momentary, because soon the right shoulder will start hurting so you will have to change it again.

And this is what your life is. You go on changing the other, thinking that perhaps this woman, this man, will bring you the paradise you have always been longing for. But everybody brings hell—without fail! Nobody is to be condemned for it, because they are doing exactly the same as you are doing: They are carrying an unreal self out of which nothing can grow. It cannot blossom. It is empty—decorated, but inside empty and hollow.

So when you see somebody from far away he or she is appealing. As you come closer, the appeal becomes less. When you meet, it is not a meeting but a clash. And suddenly you see the other person is empty, and you feel you have been deceived, cheated, because the other person has nothing that had been promised. The same is the situation of the other person regarding you. All promises fail and you become a burden to each other, a misery to each other, a sadness to each other, destructive to each other. You separate. For a little while there is relief, but your inner unreality cannot leave you in this state for long; soon you will be searching for another woman, another man, and you will get into the same trap. Only the faces are different; the inner reality is the same—empty.

If you really want to get rid of misery and suffering then you will have to understand—you don't have a self. Then it will be not just a small relief but a tremendous relief. And if you don't have a self, the need for the other disappears. It was the need of the unreal self to go on being nourished by the other. You don't need the other.

And listen carefully: When you don't need the other, you can love, and that love will not bring misery. Going beyond needs, demands, desires, love becomes a very soft sharing, a great understanding. When you understand yourself, that very day you have understood the whole of humanity. Then nobody can make you miserable. You know that they are suffering from an unreal self, and they are throwing their misery on anybody who is close by.

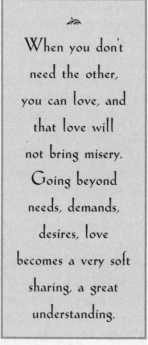

When you don't need the other, you can love, and that love will not bring misery. Going beyond needs, demands, desires, love becomes a very soft sharing, a great understanding.

Your love will make you capable of helping the person you love to get rid of the self.

I know of only one gift; love can present you with only one thing—the realization that you are not, that your "self" is just imaginary. This realization between two persons suddenly makes them one, because two nothings cannot be two. Two somethings will be two, but two nothings cannot be two. Two nothings start melting and merging. They are bound to become one.

For example, if we are sitting here, and if everybody is an ego then there are so many people; they can be counted. But there are moments when there is utter silence; then you cannot count how many people are here. There is only one consciousness, one silence, one nothingness, one selflessness. And only in that state can two persons live in eternal joy. Only in that state can any group live in tremendous beauty; the whole of humanity can live in great benediction.

But try to see the "self" and you will not find it. And not finding it is of great importance. I have told many times the story of Bodhidharma and his meeting with the Chinese emperor Wu—a very strange meeting, very fruitful. Emperor Wu perhaps was at that time the greatest emperor in the world; he ruled over all China, Mongolia, Korea, the whole of Asia except India. He became convinced of the truth of Gautam Buddha's teachings, but the people who had brought the message of Buddha were scholars. None of them were mystics. And then the news came that Bodhidharma was coming, and there was a great anticipation all over the land. Emperor Wu had become influenced by Gautam Buddha, and that meant that his whole empire was influenced by the same teaching. Now a real mystic, a buddha, was coming. It was such a great joy!

Emperor Wu had never before gone to the boundaries where India and China meet to receive anyone. With great respect he welcomed Bodhidharma, and he said, "I have been asking all the monks and the scholars who have been coming, but nobody has been of any help—I have tried everything. How to get rid of this self? Because Buddha says that unless you become a no-self, your misery cannot end."

He was sincere. Bodhidharma looked into his eyes, and he said, "I will be staying by the side of the river in the temple near the mountain. Tomorrow, at four o'clock in the morning exactly, you come and I will finish this self forever. But remember, you are not to bring any arms with you, don't bring any guards with you; you have to come alone."

Wu was a little worried—the man was strange! "How can he just destroy my self so quickly? It has been said by the scholars that it takes lives and lives of meditation; only then the self disappears. This man is weird! And he wants to meet me in the darkness, early in the morning at four o'clock, alone, without even a sword, no guards, no other companion? This man seems to be strange—he could do anything. And what does he mean that he will finish the self forever? He can kill *me,* but how will he kill the self?"

The whole night Emperor Wu could not sleep. He changed his mind again and again—to go or not to go? But there was something in Bodhidharma's eyes, there was something in his voice, and there was some aura of authority when he said, "Just come at four o'clock sharp, and I will finish this self forever! You need not be worried about it." What he had said sounded absurd, but the way he said it and the way he looked were so authoritative: He knows what he is saying. Finally Wu had to decide to go. He decided to risk it—"At the most he can kill me—what else? And I have tried everything. I cannot attain this no-self, and without attaining this no-self there is no end to misery."

He knocked on the temple door, and Bodhidharma said, "I knew you would come; I knew also that the whole night you would be changing your mind. But that does not matter—you have come. Now sit down in the lotus posture, close your eyes, and I am going to sit in front of you. The moment you find your self inside, catch hold of it so I can kill it. Just catch hold of it tightly and tell me that you have caught it, and I will kill it and it will be finished. It is a question of minutes."

Wu was a little afraid. Bodhidharma looked like a madman—he has been depicted as a madman, although he was not like that. The paintings are symbolic. That's the impression he must have left on people. It was not his real face, but that must be the face that people have remembered. He was sitting with his big staff in front of Wu, and he said to him, "Don't wait even for a second. Just the moment you catch hold of it—search inside every nook and cranny—open your eyes and then tell me that you have caught it, and I will finish it."

Then there was silence. One hour passed, two hours passed. Finally the sun was rising, and Wu was a different man. In those two hours he looked inside himself, in every nook and cranny. He had to look—that man was sitting there; he could have hit him on the head with his staff. You could expect anything, whatever, Bodhidharma was not a man of etiquette, manners; he was not part of Wu's court. So Wu had to look intently, intensively. And as he looked, he became relaxed . . . because it was nowhere! And as he looked for it, all thoughts disappeared. The search was so intense that his whole energy was involved in it; there was nothing left to think and desire, and this and that.

As the sun was rising Bodhidharma saw Wu's face; he was not the same man—such silence, such depth. He had disappeared.

Bodhidharma shook him and told him, "Open your eyes—it is not there. I don't have to kill it. I am a nonviolent man, I don't kill anything! But this self does not exist. Because you never look for it, it goes on existing. It exists only in your not looking for it, in your unawareness. Now it is gone."

Two hours had passed and Wu was immensely glad. He had never tasted such sweetness, such freshness, such newness, such beauty. And he was not. Bodhidharma had fulfilled his promise. Emperor Wu bowed down, touched his feet, and said, "Please forgive me for thinking that you are mad, thinking that you don't know manners, thinking that you are weird, thinking that you can be dangerous. I have never seen a more compassionate man than you . . . I am totally fulfilled. Now there is no question in me."

Emperor Wu said that when he died, on his grave, Bodhidharma's statement should be engraved in gold, so that the people in centuries to come would know . . . "There was a man who looked mad, but who was capable of doing miracles. Without doing anything he helped me to be a no-self. And since then everything has changed. Everything is the same but I am not the same, and life has become just a pure song of silence."

Why do I feel so much pain in letting go of the things that are caus-ing me misery?

The things that are causing you misery must be giving you some pleasure too; otherwise the question does not arise. If they were pure misery you would have dropped them. But in life, nothing is pure; everything is mixed with its opposite. Everything carries its opposite in its womb.

What you call misery, analyze it, penetrate into it, and you will see that it gives you something you would like to have. Maybe it is not yet real, maybe it is only a hope, maybe it is only a promise for tomorrow, but you will cling to the misery, you will cling to the pain, in the hope that tomorrow something that you have always desired and longed for is going to happen. You suffer misery in the hope of pleasure. If it is pure misery it is impossible to cling to it.

Just watch, be more alert about your misery. For example, you are feeling jealous. It creates misery. But look around—there must be something positive in it. It also gives you some ego, some sense of your being separate from others, some sense of superiority. Your jealousy at least pretends to be love. If you don't feel jealous you will think maybe you don't love anymore, and you are clinging to jealousy because you would like to cling to your love—at least your idea of love. If your woman or your man goes with somebody else and you don't feel jealous at all, you will immediately become con-cerned that you no longer love. Otherwise, for centuries you have been told that lovers are jealous. Jealousy has become an intrinsic part of your love: without jealousy your love dies; only with jeal-ousy can your so-called love live. If you want your love you will have to accept your jealousy and the misery that is created by it.

And your mind is very cunning and very clever in finding rationalizations. It will say, "It is natural to feel jealous." And it appears natural because everybody else is doing the same. Your mind will say, "It is natural to feel hurt when your lover leaves you, because you have loved so much! How can you avoid the hurt, the wound, when your lover leaves you?" In fact, you are enjoying your wound too, in a very subtle and unconscious way. Your wound is giving you an idea that you are a great lover, that you loved so much, that you loved so deeply. Your love was so profound, you are shattered because your lover has left you. Even if you are not shattered you will pretend to be shattered—you will believe in your own lie. You will behave as if you are in great misery, you will cry and weep—and your tears may not be true at all, but just to console yourself that you are a great lover, you have to cry and weep.

Just watch every kind of misery: Either it has some pleasure in it which you are not ready to lose, or it has some hope in it which goes on dangling in front of you like a carrot. And it looks so close, just by the corner, and you have traveled so long and now the goal is so close—why drop it? You will find some rationalization in it, some hypocrisy in it.

Just a few days ago a woman wrote to me that her man has left her and she is not feeling miserable—she wants to know what is wrong with her? "Why am I not feeling miserable? Am I too hard, rocklike? I don't feel any misery," she wrote to me. She is miserable because she is not feeling misery! She was expecting to be shattered. "On the contrary," she wrote, "I can confess that I am feeling happy—and that makes me very sad. What kind of love is this? I am feeling happy, unburdened; a great load has disappeared from my being." She asked me, "Is it

> Just watch every kind of misery: Either it has some pleasure in it which you are not ready to lose, or it has some hope in it which goes on dangling in front of you like a carrot.

normal? Am I all right or is something basically wrong with me?"

Nothing is wrong with her, she is absolutely right. In fact, when lovers—after a long togetherness and all the misery that is bound to happen when you are together—leave each other, it is a relief. But it is against the ego to confess that it is a relief. For a few days at least you will move with a long face, with tears flowing from your eyes— phony, but this is the idea that has prevailed in the world.

If somebody dies and you don't feel sad you will start feeling that something is certainly wrong with you. How can you avoid sadness when somebody has died? Because we have been told it is natural, it is normal, and everybody wants to be natural and normal. It is not normal, it is only average. It is not natural, it is only a long-cultivated habit; otherwise there is nothing to weep and cry about. Death destroys nothing. The body is dust and falls into dust, and the consciousness has two possibilities: If it still has desires then it will move into another womb, or if all the desires have disappeared then it will move into the womb of existence, into eternity. Nothing is destroyed. The body again becomes part of the earth, goes into rest, and the soul moves into the universal consciousness or moves into another body.

But you cry and weep and you carry your sadness for many days. It is just a formality—or if it is not a formality then there is every possibility that you never loved the person who has died and now you are feeling repentant. You never loved the person totally and now there is no more time. Now the person has disappeared, now they will never be available. Maybe you had quarreled with your husband and he died in the night in his sleep—now you will say you are crying because he has died, but really you are crying because you have not even been able to ask his forgiveness. You have not even been able to say good-bye. The quarrel will hang over you like a cloud forever.

If you live moment to moment in totality, then there is never any repentance, no guilt. If you have loved totally, there is no question. One day if the lover leaves, it simply means that now our ways are parting. We can say good-bye, we can be thankful to each other. We shared so much, we loved so much, we have enriched each other's lives so much—what is there to cry and weep about, and why be miserable?

But people are so entangled in their rationalizations that they can't see beyond them. And they rationalize everything. Even things that are obviously simple become very complicated.

You ask me, "Why do I feel so much pain in letting go of the things that are causing me misery?" You are not yet convinced that they are causing you misery. I am saying that they are causing you misery, but you are not yet convinced. And it is not a question of *my* saying it—the basic thing is that *you* will have to understand: "These are the things that are causing me misery." And you will have to see that there are investments in your misery. If you want those investments you will have to learn to live with the misery; if you want to drop the misery, you will have to drop those investments too.

Have you observed it? If you talk about your misery to people, they give sympathy to you. Everybody is sympathetic to the miserable man. Now, if you love getting sympathy from people you cannot drop your misery; that is your investment.

> If you have loved totally, there is no question. One day if the lover leaves, that simply means now our ways are parting. We can say goodbye, we can be thankful to each other.

The miserable husband comes home, the wife is loving, sympathetic. The more miserable he is, the more his children are considerate of him; the more miserable he is, the more his friends are friendly toward him. Everybody takes care of him. The moment he starts becoming happy they withdraw their sympathy, of course—a happy person needs no sympathy. The happier he is, the more he finds that nobody cares about him. It is as if everybody becomes suddenly hard, frozen. Now, how can you drop your misery?

You will have to drop this desire for attention, this desire for getting sympathy from people. In fact, it is very ugly to desire sympathy from people—it makes you a beggar. And remember, sympathy is not love; they are obliging you, they are fulfilling a kind of duty—it is not love. They may not like you, but still they will sympathize with you. This is etiquette, culture, civilization, formality—but you are living on false things. Your misery is real and what you are getting in the bargain is false. Of course, if you become happy, if you drop your miseries, it will be a radical change in your lifestyle; things may start changing.

Once a woman came to me, the wife of one of the richest men in India, and she told me, "I want to meditate, but my husband is against it."

I asked her, "Why is your husband against meditation?"

She said, "He says, 'The way you are, I love you. I don't know what will happen after meditation. If you start meditating you are bound to change; then I don't know whether I will be able to love you or not, because you will be another person.'"

I said to the woman, "Your husband has a point there—certainly things will be different. You will be more free, more independent. You will be more joyous, and your husband will have to learn to live with a new woman. He may not like you that way, he may start feeling inferior. Right now he feels superior to you."

I told the woman, "Your husband is right; before you enter on the path of meditation you have to consider it, because there are dangers ahead."

She didn't listen to me; she started meditating. Now she is divorced. She came to see me after a few years and said, "You were right. The more silent I became, the more my husband became furious at me. He was never so violent—something strange started happening," she told me. "The more silent and quiet I was becoming, the more aggressive he was becoming." His whole male chauvinist mind was at stake. He wanted to destroy the peace and the silence that was happening to the woman so he could remain superior. And because it could not happen the way he wanted, he divorced the woman.

It is a very strange world! If you become peaceful, your relationships with people will change because you are a different person. If your relationship was tied to your misery, the relationship may disappear.

I used to have a friend. He was a professor in the same university where I was a professor; he was a great social worker. In India, what to do with the widows is still a problem. Nobody wants to marry them, and widows are not in favor of marrying either; it seems like a sin. And this professor was determined to marry a widow. He was not concerned whether he was in love with the woman or not—that was secondary, irrelevant—his only interest was that she should be a widow. And he persuaded one woman, slowly, and she was ready.

I told the man, "Before you take the plunge, consider it for at least three days—go into isolation. Are you in love with the woman, or is it just a great social service that you are doing?" Marrying a widow in India is thought to be something very revolutionary, something radical. "Are you just trying to

> If you become peaceful, your relationship with people will change because you are a different person. If your relationship was because of your misery, the relationship may disappear.

prove that you are a revolutionary? If you are trying to prove that you are a revolutionary, then you are bound for trouble—the moment you are married she will no longer be a widow and your interest will be gone."

He didn't listen to me. He got married . . . and after six months he told me, "You were right." He cried. He said, "I could not see the point: I was in love with her widowhood, not in love with her for herself, and now certainly she is no longer a widow."

So I said, "You do one thing—commit suicide, make her a widow again, and give somebody else a chance to be a revolutionary!" What else can you do?

Man's mind is so stupid, so unconscious. It is in deep sleep, slumber, snoring.

You cannot let go of things that are causing you misery because you have not yet seen the investments, you have not yet looked deeply into them. You have not seen that there is some pleasure you are deriving out of your misery. You will have to drop both—and then there is no problem. In fact, misery and pleasure can only be dropped together. And then what arises is bliss.

Bliss is not pleasure. Bliss is not even happiness. Happiness is always bound together with unhappiness and pleasure is always bound together with pain. Dropping both . . . You want to drop misery so that you can be happy—that is an absolutely wrong approach. You will have to drop both. Seeing that they are together, one drops them; you cannot choose one part.

In life, everything has an organic unity. Pain and pleasure are not two things. Really, if we make a more scientific language, we will drop these words: pain and pleasure. We will make one word: pain-pleasure, happinessunhappiness, daynight, lifedeath. These are each one word because they are inseparable. And you want to choose one part: You want to have only the roses and not the thorns, you want only the day and not the night, you want only love and not hate. This is not going to happen—this is not the way things are. You will have to drop both, and then arises a totally different world: the world of bliss.

Bliss is absolute peace, neither disturbed by pain nor disturbed by pleasure.

To celebrate their fortieth anniversary, Seymour and Rose went back to the same second-floor hotel room where they had spent their honeymoon.

"Now," said Seymour, "just like that first night, let us undress, get in opposite corners of the room, turn off the lights, then run to each other and embrace." They undressed, went to opposite corners, switched off the lights and ran toward each other. But their sense of direction was dulled by forty years, so Seymour missed Rose and he went right through the window. He landed on the lawn in a daze.

Seymour tapped on the lobby window to get the clerk's attention. "I fell down from upstairs," he said. "I am naked and I gotta get back to my room."

"It's okay," said the clerk. "Nobody will see you."

"Are you crazy? I gotta walk through the lobby and I am all naked!"

"Nobody can see you," repeated the clerk. "Everybody is upstairs trying to get some old lady off a door-knob!"

People are so foolish! Not only the younger ones—the older you get, the more foolish you become. The more experienced you are, it seems the more stupidity you accumulate through life. It really rarely happens that a person starts watching, observing his own life and his own life patterns.

See what your misery is, what desires are causing it, and why you are clinging to those desires. And it is not for the first time that you are clinging to those desires; this has been the pattern of your whole life and you have not arrived anywhere. You go on in circles, you never come to any real growth. You remain childish, stupid. You are born with the intelligence that can make you a buddha, but it is lost in unnecessary things.

A farmer who had only two impotent old bulls bought a new, young, vigorous bull. Immediately the stud began mounting one cow after another in the pasture. After watching this for an hour, one of the ancient bulls started pawing the ground and snorting.

"What's the matter?" asked the other. "You getting young ideas?"

"No," said the first bull, "but I don't want that young fellow to think I am one of the cows."

Even in their old age people go on carrying their egos. They have to pretend, they have to pose, and their whole life is nothing but a long story of misery. Still they defend it. Rather than being ready to change it, they are very defensive.

Drop all defensiveness, drop all armor. Start watching how you live your day-to-day life, moment to moment. And whatever you are doing, go into its details. You need not go to a psychoanalyst, you can analyze each pattern of your life yourself—it is such a simple process! Just watch and you will be able to see what is happening, what has been happening. You have been choosing, and that has been the problem—you have been choosing one part against the other, and they are both together. Don't choose at all. Just watch and be aware without choosing, and you will find yourself in paradise.

Should one first come to terms with one's own loneliness before entering into relationship?

Yes, you have to come to terms with your loneliness, so much so that the loneliness is transformed into aloneness. Only then will you be capable of moving into a deep, enriching relationship. Only then will you be able to move into love. What do I mean when I say that one has to come to terms with one's loneliness, so much so that it becomes aloneness?

Loneliness is a negative state of mind. Aloneness is positive, notwithstanding what the dictionaries say. In dictionaries, loneliness and aloneness are synonymous—in life they are not. Loneliness is a state of mind when you are constantly missing the other. Aloneness is the state of mind when you are constantly delighted in yourself. Loneliness is miserable. Aloneness is blissful. Loneliness is always worried, missing something, hankering for something, desiring something. Aloneness is a deep fulfillment, not going out, tremendously content, happy, celebrating. In loneliness you are off center. In aloneness you are centered and rooted. Aloneness is beautiful. It has an elegance about it, a grace, a climate of tremendous satisfaction. Loneliness is beggarly; all around it there is begging and nothing else. It has no grace about it, in fact it is ugly. Loneliness is a dependence, aloneness is sheer independence. One feels as if one is one's whole world, one's whole existence.

Now, if you move into a relationship when you are feeling lonely, then you will exploit the other. The other will become a means to satisfy you. You will use the other, and everybody resents being used because nobody is here to become a means for anybody else. Every human being is an end unto himself or herself. Nobody is here to be used like a thing, everybody is here to be worshiped like a king. Nobody is here to fulfill anybody else's expectations, everybody is here just to be himself, to be herself. So whenever you move into any relationship out of loneliness, the relationship is already on the rocks. Even before it has started, it is already on the rocks. Even before the birth, the child is dead. It is going to create more misery for you. And remember, when you move according to your loneliness you will fall into a relationship with somebody who is in the same plight, because nobody who is really living his or her aloneness will be attracted to you. You will be too far below them. They can at the most sympathize, but cannot love you. One who is on the peak of aloneness can only be attracted toward someone who is also alone. So whenever you act according to your loneliness, you will find a person of the same type; you will find your own reflection somewhere. Two beggars will meet, two miserable people will meet. And remember—when two miserable people meet, it is not a simple addition, it is a multiplication. They create much more misery for each other than they could have created in their loneliness.

First become alone. First start enjoying yourself, first love yourself. First become so authentically happy that if nobody comes it doesn't matter. You are full, overflowing. If nobody knocks at your door it is perfectly okay—you are not missing anything. You are not waiting for somebody to come and knock at the door. You are at home—if somebody comes, good, beautiful. If nobody comes, that too is beautiful and good. *Then* move into a relationship. Now you move like a master, not like a beggar. Now you move like an emperor, not like a beggar.

And the person who has lived in his aloneness will always be attracted to another person who is also living his aloneness beautifully, because like attracts like. When two masters meet—masters of their beings, of their aloneness—happiness is not just added, it is multiplied. It becomes a tremendous phenomenon of celebration. And they don't exploit, they share. They don't use each other. On the contrary, they become one and enjoy the existence that surrounds them.

Two lonely people are always facing each other, confronting

each other. Two people together who have known aloneness are facing something higher than both. I always give this example: Two ordinary lovers who are both lonely always face each other; two real lovers, on a full-moon night, will not be facing each other. They may be holding hands, but they will be facing the full moon high in the sky. They will not be facing each other, they will be together facing something else. Sometimes they will be listening to a symphony by Mozart or Beethoven or Wagner together. Sometimes they will be sitting by the side of a tree and enjoying the tremendous being of the tree enveloping them. Sometimes they may be sitting by a waterfall and listening to the wild music that is continuously being created there. Sometimes, by the ocean, they will both be looking to the farthest possibility that the eyes can see. Whenever two lonely persons meet, they look at each other, because they are constantly in search of ways and means to exploit the other—how to use the other, how to be happy through the other. But two persons who are deeply contented within themselves are not trying to use each other.

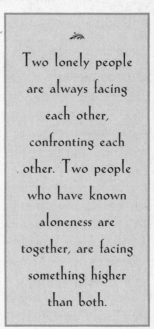

Two lonely people are always facing each other, confronting each other. Two people who have known aloneness are together, are facing something higher than both.

Rather, they become fellow travelers; they move on a pilgrimage. The goal is high, the goal is far away. Their common interest joins them together.

Ordinarily the common interest is sex. Sex can join two persons momentarily and casually, and very superficially. Real lovers have a greater common interest. It is not that there will be no sex; there may be, but as part of a higher harmony. Listening to

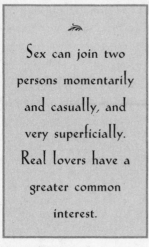

Sex can join two persons momentarily and casually, and very superficially. Real lovers have a greater common interest.

Mozart's or Beethoven's symphony, they may come so close, so close, so close, that they may make love to each other, but it is in the greater harmony of a Beethoven symphony. The symphony was the real thing; the love happens as part of it. And when love happens of its own accord, unsought, unthought, simply happens as part of a higher harmony, it has a totally different quality to it. It is divine, it is no longer human.

The word *happiness* comes from a Scandanavian word, *hap*. The word *happening* also comes from the same root. Happiness is that which happens. You cannot produce it, you cannot command it, you cannot force it. At the most you can be available to it. Whenever it happens, it happens.

Two real lovers are always available but never thinking about—never trying to find—happiness. Then they are never frustrated, because whenever it happens it happens. They create the situation—in fact, if you are happy with yourself, you are already the situation, and if the other is also happy with himself or herself, she is also the situation. When these two situations come close, a greater situation is created. In that greater situation much happens—nothing is done.

Man has not to do anything to be happy. Man has just to flow and let go.

So, the question is: "Should one first come to terms with one's own loneliness before entering into a relationship?" Yes—yes, absolutely. It has to be so, otherwise you will be frustrated, and in the name of love you will be doing something else, which is not love at all.

Is this really all there is? My life seems so meaningless and empty. I keep thinking there must be something more. I want there to be something more.

There is infinitely more, but your wanting it is a barrier in reaching it. Desiring is like a wall that surrounds you; nondesiring becomes a door.

This is one of the most paradoxical but very fundamental laws of life: Desire and you will miss, don't desire and it is yours.

Jesus says: Seek and ye shall find. Buddha says: Seek ye not; otherwise you will miss. Jesus says: Ask and it shall be given to you. Buddha says: Ask not; otherwise it will never be given to you. Jesus says: Knock and the doors shall be opened. Buddha says: Wait . . . look . . . the doors are not closed at all. If you knock, your very knocking shows that you are knocking somewhere else—on the wall—because the doors are always open.

Jesus is as enlightened as Buddha—because there is no question of being more enlightened or less enlightened. So why this difference? The difference comes from the people to whom Jesus is speaking. He is speaking to people who are uninitiated, uninitiated into the mysteries of life. Buddha is speaking to a totally different kind of group—the initiates, the adepts, those who can understand the paradoxical. The paradoxical means the mysterious.

You say, "My life seems so meaningless and empty . . ." It seems so meaningless and empty because you are constantly hankering for more. Drop that hankering, and then you will go through a radical transformation. The emptiness disappears immediately as you stop asking for more. The emptiness is a by-product of asking for more, it is a shadow that follows the desire for more. Let the desire disappear and look back—there is no shadow anymore.

Asking for more is what our mind *is*—a constant asking for more. It makes no difference how much you have, the mind will go on asking for more. And because it goes on asking for more you go

> *Asking for more is what our mind is—a constant asking for more. It makes no difference how much you have, the mind will go on asking for more.*

on feeling you are empty, you are missing so much. See the point? The emptiness is created by asking for more. The emptiness is not there, it is a fallacy, but it will look very real when you are caught in the net of desiring.

See that desire is the cause of your emptiness. Watch your desiring, and in watching it disappears—and with it, the emptiness disappears. Then comes a deep fulfillment. You feel so full that you start overflowing. You have so much that you start sharing, you start giving—giving for the sheer joy of giving, for no other reason. You become like a cloud full of rainwater: It has to shower somewhere. It will shower even on the rocks where nothing is going to grow; it will shower unconditionally. It will not ask whether this is the right place to shower or not. It will be so burdened with rainwater that it *has* to shower to unburden itself.

When desiring disappears you are so full of bliss, so full of contentment, so full of *fullness*, that you start sharing. It happens on its own. And then there is meaning in life, then there is significance in life. Then there is poetry, beauty, grace. Then there is music, harmony—your life becomes a dance.

This emptiness and meaninglessness is your doing, so you can undo it. You say, "I keep thinking there must be something more." That's what is creating the trouble. And I am not saying there is not something more, there is—much more than you can ever imagine. I have seen it, I have heard it, I have experienced it—there is infinitely more! But you will never come into contact with it if desiring continues. Desiring is a wall, no-desiring is a bridge. Bliss is a state of no-desire, misery is a state of desire.

You say, "I want there to be something more." The more you want the more you will miss. You can choose. If you want to remain miserable, want more, more and more, and you will be missing more and more. This is your choice, remember, this is your responsibility. Nobody is forcing you. If you really want to see that which is, don't hanker for the future, for more. Just see to that which is.

Mind is constantly asking, desiring, demanding, and creating frustration because it lives in expectations. The whole world is suffering from feelings of meaninglessness, and the reason is that man is asking for more than he has ever asked before. For the first time man is desiring more than he has ever desired. Science has given him so much hope, so much support for desiring more. In the beginning of the twentieth century there was great optimism all over the world because science was opening new doors and everybody was thinking, "The golden age has arrived, it is just around the corner. We have reached it. In our very lifetime we will see that paradise has descended on the earth." Naturally everybody started desiring more and more and more.

Paradise has not descended on the earth. Instead, the earth has become a hell. Science released your desiring, it supported your desires. It supported your hopes that those desires could be fulfilled. And the outcome is that the whole world is living in deep misery. It has never been so before. It is very strange, because for the first time man has more possessions than ever. For the first time man has more safety, more security, more scientific technology, more comfort than ever before. But there is also more meaninglessness. Man has never been in such despair, in such a desperate effort to get more.

Science gives you desiring; meditation gives you an insight into desiring. That insight helps you to drop desire. And then suddenly something that was hidden up to now becomes unhidden, becomes manifest. Something wells up within your being, and everything that you had ever desired is fulfilled . . . and more. More is available than you could have imagined, than anybody has ever imagined. Unimaginable bliss descends on you. But prepare the ground. Prepare the right soil. Not-desiring is the name of the right soil.

Just be in a receptive mood. You are aggressive—you want more, that is a subtle aggression. Be receptive, open, available . . . then you are entitled to all the miracles possible.

I feel caught. The frustration of boredom only increases when I think that anything I might do is a meaningless frenzy. What exactly is boredom?

Boredom is one of the most important things in human life. Only man is capable of boredom; no other animal is capable of being bored. Boredom exists only when the mind starts coming closer and closer to enlightenment. Boredom is just the polar opposite of enlightenment. Animals cannot become enlightened, hence they cannot become bored either.

Boredom simply shows that you are becoming aware of the futility of life, its constant repetitive wheel. You have done all those things before—nothing happens. You have been into all those trips before—nothing comes out of it. Boredom is the first indication that a great understanding is arising in you about the futility, meaninglessness, of life and its ways.

Now, you can respond to boredom in two ways. One way is what people ordinarily do: escape from it, avoid it, don't look at it eye to eye, don't encounter it. Keep it at your back and run away; run into things which can occupy you, which can become obsessions; which take you so far away from the realities of life that you never see boredom arising again.

That's why people have invented alcohol, drugs. They are ways to escape from boredom. But you cannot really escape; you can only avoid for a while. Again and again the boredom will be coming, and again and again it will be more and more loud. You can escape in sex, in eating too much, in music—in a thousand and one kinds of things you can escape. But again and again the boredom will arise. It is not something that can be avoided; it is part of human growth. It has to be faced.

The other response is to face it, to meditate on it, to be with it, to be it. That's what Buddha was doing under the bodhi tree— that's what all Zen people have been doing down the ages.

What exactly is meditation? Facing boredom is meditation. What does a meditator go on doing? Sitting silently, looking at his own navel, or watching his breathing, he is being entertained by these things, do you think? He is utterly bored! That's why the Zen master moves with a stick in his hand—because those bored people are bound to fall asleep. There is no other escape, so only one escape is left: at least they can fall asleep. They cannot escape. They have themselves, of their own accord, become part of the Zen training and the discipline—they cannot escape. But one escape is always available: You can fall asleep, then you forget all about it. That's why in meditation one feels sleepy.

The whole effort in meditation is this: Be bored but don't escape from it; and keep alert, because if you fall asleep you have escaped. Keep alert! Watch it, witness it. If it is there, then it is there. It has to be looked into, to the very core of it.

If you go on looking into boredom without escaping, the explosion comes. One day, suddenly, looking deep into boredom, you penetrate your own nothingness. Boredom is just the cover, the container in which is contained your inner nothingness. If you escape from boredom, you are escaping from your own nothingness. If you don't escape from boredom, if you start living with it, if you start accepting it, welcoming it . . . That's what meditation is all about: welcoming boredom, going into it on one's own; not waiting for it to come but searching for it.

Sitting for hours in a yoga posture, just watching one's breathing, one gets utterly bored. And the whole training of meditation is such that it helps boredom. In a Zen monastery you have to get up every day at the same time in the morning—every day, year in, year out. It doesn't matter whether it is summer or winter. You have to get up early, three o'clock, you have to take a bath. You have to drink the same tea, and you have to sit . . . The same gestures followed again and again. And the whole day is also a very fixed routine: You will eat your breakfast at a certain time, then you will meditate again, then you will have your food at a certain time—and the same food! Everything helps boredom.

And the same clothes, the same monastery, and the same master every day with his stick walking around. Every day in the evening you have to go for a session with the master. And the questions that are given are such boring questions to meditate on: "What is the sound of one hand clapping?" Just think of if—it will drive you mad! What is the sound of one hand clapping? There is no answer to it, you know it; everybody knows there is no answer to it. And the master goes on insisting, "Go on repeating, go on meditating on it."

It is all well managed. The boredom has to be created—immensely, tremendously. The boredom has to be allowed as totally as possible, has to be helped, supported from every side. The same evening, the same work, the same chanting of the mantra. The same time you have to go to sleep again . . . and this goes on, this wheel. Within a few days you are utterly bored and you cannot escape. There is no way to escape. You can't go to the movies, you can't watch TV; you can't have anything that will help you to avoid it. You are thrown into it again and again.

Great courage is needed to face it. It is almost like death; in fact, far harder than death, because death comes when you go unconscious.

And you are stirring up all sorts of boredom. What happens? This is the secret of all meditations: If you go on watching, watching, watching, boredom becomes bigger and bigger, more and more intense, and then the peak. Nothing can go on forever—there is a point where the wheel turns. If you can go to the very extreme, to the very peak, then the change, transformation—enlightenment, satori, or whatever you want to call it—happens. Then one day, suddenly, the boredom becomes too much. You are suffocated, you are almost being killed by it. You are surrounded by an ocean of boredom. You are overwhelmed by it and there seems to be no way to escape. The very intensity and totality of it, and the wheel turns. Suddenly boredom disappears and there is *satori*, samadhi. You have entered your nothingness.

Now there will be no boredom anymore. You have seen the very nothingness of life. You have disappeared—who can be bored? With what? You exist no more. You are annihilated.

You ask: "What exactly is boredom?"

A great spiritual phenomenon. That's why buffaloes are not bored; they look perfectly happy and joyous. Only man is bored. And in man, also, only the people who are very talented and intelligent are bored. The stupid people are not bored. They are perfectly happy doing their jobs, earning money, creating a bigger bank balance, raising their children, reproducing, eating, sitting in the movie theater, going to the restaurant, participating in this and that. They are enjoying! They are not bored. They are the lowest types; they really belong to the world of buffaloes. They are not yet human.

A man becomes human when he starts feeling bored. You can see it: The most intelligent child will be the most bored child—because nothing can keep his interest for long. Sooner or later he stumbles upon the fact and asks, "Now what? What next? This is finished. I have seen this toy, I have looked into it, I have opened it, I have analyzed it, now I am finished—what is next?" By the time he becomes a youth, he is already bored.

Buddha was utterly bored. He left his kingdom when he was only twenty-nine, at the peak of his youth. He was utterly bored—with women, with wine, with wealth, with kingdom, with everything. He had seen all, he had seen through and through. He was bored. He renounced the world not because the world is wrong, remember. Traditionally it is said he renounced the world because the world is bad—that is absolute nonsense. He renounced the world because he became so bored with it.

It is not bad, neither is it good. If you are intelligent, it is boredom. If you are stupid, you can go on. Then it is a merry-go-round; then you move from one sensation to another. You are interested in trivia and you go on repeating and you are not conscious enough to see the repetition—you can't see that yesterday you were doing this, and today also, and you are imagining to do the same thing again tomorrow. You must be really unintelligent. How can intelligence avoid boredom? It is impossible. Intelligence means seeing things as they are.

Buddha left the world out of boredom; utterly bored, he ran away from the world. And what was he doing then for six years sitting in those forests? He was getting more and more bored. What can you do, sitting in a forest? Watch your breath, look at your navel, day in, day out, year in, year out. He created that boredom to its ultimate peak, and one night it disappeared. It disappeared of its own accord.

If you reach to the peak . . . the turn comes. It comes! And with that turn of the tide, light enters your being—you disappear, only light remains. And with light comes delight. You are full of joy—you are *not*, but full of joy for no reason at all. Joy simply bubbles up in your being.

The ordinary person is joyous for a reason—he has fallen in love with a new woman or a new man and he is joyous. His joy is momentary. Tomorrow he will be fed up with this woman and he will start looking for another. The ordinary man is joyous because he has got a new car; tomorrow he will have to look for another car. It goes on and on . . . and he never sees the point of it, that always, finally, one is bored. Do whatever—finally you are bored, every act brings boredom. The intelligent person sees it. The sooner you see it the more intelligence you show.

Then what is left? Then only boredom is left, and one has to meditate over it. There is no way to escape from it. Then go into it, see where it leads. And if you can keep going into it, it leads into enlightenment.

Only man is capable of boredom, and only man is capable of enlightenment.

Can you say something about the drug problem? What makes people get involved in using drugs?

It is nothing new, it is as ancient as man. There has never been a time when man was not in search of escape. The most ancient book in the world is the *Rigveda,* and it is full of drug use. The name of the drug is *soma.*

Since those ancient times all the religions have tried to get people not to use drugs. All the governments have been against drugs. Yet drugs have proved more powerful than governments or religions, because nobody has looked into the very psychology of the drug user. Man is miserable. He lives in anxiety, anguish, and frustration. There seems to be no way out except drugs.

The only way to prevent the use of drugs will be to make people joyful, happy, blissful.

I am also against drugs, for the simple reason that they help you to forget your misery for a time. They do not prepare you to fight misery and suffering; rather, they weaken you.

But the reasons of religions and governments for being against drugs and my reasons for being against drugs are totally different.

They want people to remain miserable and frustrated, because those who are in suffering are never rebellious; they are tortured in their own beings, they are falling apart. They cannot conceive of a better society, of a better culture, of a better human being. Because of this misery, anybody can become an easy victim of the priests, because they will console him, they say to him, "Blessed are the poor, blessed are the meek, blessed are those who suffer, because they shall inherit the kingdom of God."

The suffering humanity is also in the hands of the politicians, because the suffering humanity needs some hope—the hope of a classless society somewhere in the future, the hope of a society where there will be no poverty, no hunger, no misery. In short, people can manage and be patient with their sufferings if they have a utopia just on the horizon. And you must note the meaning of the word *utopia*. It means "that which never happens." It is just like the horizon; it is so close that you think you can run and meet the place where earth and sky meet. But you can go on running your whole life and never meet the place, because there is no such place. It is a hallucination.

The politician lives on promises, the priest lives on promises. In the last ten thousand years nobody has delivered the goods. Their reason for being against drugs is that drugs destroy their whole business. If people start taking opium, hashish, LSD, they won't care about communism, and they won't care about what is going to happen tomorrow; they won't care about life after death, they won't care about God, paradise. They will be fulfilled in the moment.

Here my reasons are different. I am also against drugs, not because they cut the roots of the religions and the politicians but because they destroy your inner growth toward spirituality. They prevent you from reaching the promised land. You remain hanging around the hallucinations, while you are capable of reaching the real. They give you a toy.

But since drugs are not going to disappear, I would like every government, every scientific lab, to purify drugs, to make them healthier without any side effects, which is possible now. We can create a drug like the one Aldous Huxley, in memory of the *Rigveda*, called "soma"—which will be without any bad effects, which will not be addictive, which will be a joy, a happiness, a dance, a song.

If we cannot make it possible for everybody to become a Gautam Buddha, we have no right to prevent people from at least having illusory glimpses of the aesthetic state that Gautam Buddha must have had. Perhaps these small experiences will lead the person to explore more. Sooner or later he is going to be fed up with the drug, because it will go on repeating the same scene again and again. However beautiful a scene is, repetition makes it boring.

So first purify the drug from all bad effects. Second, let people who want to enjoy, enjoy. They will become bored by it. And then their only path will be to seek some method of meditation to find the ultimate bliss.

The question is basically concerned with younger people. The generation gap is the world's very latest phenomenon; it never used to exist. In the past, children of six and seven started using their hands, their minds, with their fathers in their traditional professions. By the time they were fourteen they were already craftsmen, workers, they were married, they had responsibilities. By the time they were twenty or twenty-four they had their own children, so there was never a gap between the generations. Each generation overlapped the other generation.

For the first time in the history of humanity the generation gap has appeared. It is of tremendous importance. Now, for the first time, up to the age of twenty-five or twenty-six when you come back from the university you have no responsibility—no children, no worries, and you have the whole world before you to dream about. How to better it, how to make it richer, how to create a race of geniuses. These are the years, between fourteen and twenty-four, when one is a dreamer, because sexuality is maturing, and with sexuality dreams are maturing. One's sexuality is repressed by the schools and colleges, so the young person's whole energy is available to dream. He becomes a communist, he becomes a socialist, he becomes a Fabian, all sorts of things. And this is the time when he starts feeling frustrated because of the way the world works. The bureaucracy, the government, the politicians, the society, the religion . . . it does not seem that he will be able to make his dreams a reality. He comes home from the university full of ideas, and every idea is going to be crushed by the society. Soon he forgets about the new human being and the new age. He cannot even find employment, he cannot feed himself. How can he think about a classless society where there will be no rich and no poor?

It is this moment when he turns toward drugs. They give him temporary relief; but soon he finds that he has to go on increasing the dose. And as drugs are now, they are destructive to the body, to the brain; soon he is absolutely helpless. He cannot live without drugs, and with drugs there is no space in life for him.

But I don't say that the younger people are responsible for it, and to punish them and put them in jail is sheer stupidity. They are not criminals, they are victims.

My idea is that education should be divided into two parts: one intellectual and the other practical. From the very beginning, a child enters school not just to learn the three R's, but also to learn to create something—some craft, some skill. Half of the time should be given to his intellectual pursuits, and half of the time should be given to life's real necessities; that will keep the balance. And by the time he comes out of the university, he will not be a utopian, and he will not be in need of employment by others. He will be able to create things on his own.

And for students who feel any kind of frustration, from the very beginning things should be changed. If they are frustrated perhaps they are not studying the right things. Perhaps they want to become a carpenter and you are making them a doctor; they want to become a gardener and you are making them an engineer.

Great psychological understanding will be needed so that each child is sent in the direction where he will learn something. And in every school, every college, every university, at least one hour of meditation for everybody must be compulsory, so that whenever he feels frustrated or depressed he has a space within himself that he can move to, and immediately get rid of all the depression and frustration. He need not turn to drugs. Meditation is the answer.

But rather than doing all these things, the people who are in power go on doing idiotic things—prohibition, punishment. They know that for ten thousand years we have been prohibiting and we have not succeeded. If you prohibit alcohol more people become alcoholics, and a dangerous kind of alcohol becomes available. Thousands of people die by poisoning, and who is responsible?

Now they are punishing young people for years in jail without even understanding that if a person has taken a drug or has been addicted to a drug he needs treatment, not punishment. He should be sent to a place where he can be taken care of, where he can be taught meditation, and slowly, slowly, can be directed away from the drugs toward something better.

Instead they are forcing them into jails—years in jail! They don't value human life at all. If you give ten years in jail to a young man of twenty you have wasted his most precious time—and without any benefit, because in jail every drug is more easily available than anywhere else. The inmates are all highly skilled drug users, who become teachers for those who are amateurs. After ten years the person will come out perfectly trained. Your jails teach only one thing: Anything you do is not wrong unless you are caught; just don't be caught. And there are masters who can teach you how not to be caught again. So this whole thing is absolutely absurd.

I am also against drugs, but in a totally different way. I think you can understand the point.

How can we be so concerned with our own happiness when there are so many problems that face humankind? Hunger, poverty, miserable living conditions, so little opportunity for most people to develop their abilities and talents . . .

In fact, before you have dropped your own problems, you cannot have the right perspective to understand the world's problems. Your own home is in such a mess, your own inner being is in such a mess—how can you have the perspective to understand vast problems? You have not even understood yourself—start from there, because every other start will be a wrong start.

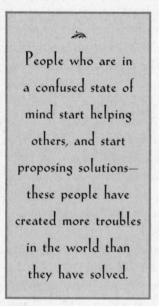

People who are in a confused state of mind start helping others, and start proposing solutions—these people have created more troubles in the world than they have solved.

People who are in a tremendously confused state of mind start helping others, and start proposing solutions—these people have created more troubles in the world than they have solved. These are the real mischief-makers: the politicians, the economists, the so-called public servants, missionaries. These are the real mischief-makers—they have not solved their own inner consciousness yet, and they are ready to jump on everybody else and solve everybody else's problems. In fact, in this way they are avoiding their own reality—they don't want to face it. They want to remain engaged somewhere else with somebody else. This gives them something to do, it is a good distraction.

Remember: *you* are the world problem. *You* are the problem, and unless *you* are solved, whatever you do is going to make things more complicated. First put your own house in order, create a cosmos there—it is a chaos.

There is an ancient Indian fable, a very old story but of great importance:

A great but foolish king complained that the rough ground hurt his feet, so he ordered that the whole kingdom be carpeted with cowhide to protect his feet. But the court fool laughed at the idea—he was a wise man. Said he, "The king's idea is simply ridiculous."

The king was very angry and said to the fool, "You show me a better alternative, otherwise you will be put to death."

The fool said, "Sire, cut out small pads of cowhide to cover your feet." And this is how shoes were born.

There is no need to cover the whole earth with cowhide; just covering your own feet covers the whole earth. This is the beginning of wisdom.

Yes, there are problems, I agree. There are great problems. Life is such a hell. Misery is there, poverty is there, violence is there, all kinds of madnesses are afloat, that's true—but still I insist the problem arises in the individual soul. The problem is there because individuals are in chaos. The overall chaos is nothing but a combined phenomenon: We have all poured our chaos into it.

The world is nothing but a relationship; we are related with each other. I am neurotic, you are neurotic: then the relationship goes very, very neurotic—multiplied, not only doubled. And everybody *is* neurotic, hence the world is neurotic. Adolf Hitler is not born out of the blue—we create him. War is not born out of the blue—we create it. It is our pus that comes out; it is our chaos that takes the toll. The beginning has to be with you: You are the

world problem. So don't avoid the reality of your inner world—
that is the first thing.

As you are now, you cannot see the root of a problem, you see
only the symptom. First find out within yourself where the root is,
and try hard to change that root. Poverty is not the root—greed is
the root, poverty is the outcome. You go on fighting with poverty
and nothing will happen. Greed is the root; the greed has to be
uprooted. War is not the problem, individual aggressiveness is the
problem—war is just the sum total of individual aggression. You go
on making protest marches and war is not going to be stopped.
There are a few people who enjoy the fun; you can find them in
any protest march.

In my childhood, I used to enjoy it very much. I was in every
procession, and even the elders of my town started worrying. They
said, "You are everywhere—whether it is a communist procession
or socialist or anticommunist . . . you are there." I said, "I enjoy the
fun. I'm not concerned with the political philosophy—just shout-
ing is so much fun; I enjoy the exercise." You can enjoy; it does not
make much difference—war goes on. And if you look at these pro-
testers you will see these are very aggressive people—you will not
see peace on their faces. They are ready to fight. Peace marches can
any moment turn into riots. These are aggressive people—in the
name of peace they are showing their aggression. They are ready to
fight: If they had power, if they had the atom bomb, they would
drop the bomb to create peace. That's what all the politicians say—
they say they are fighting so that peace can prevail.

The problem is not war, and protest marches are not going to
help. The problem is inner aggression in individuals. People are not
at ease within themselves, hence war has to exist, otherwise these
people will go mad. Each decade a great war is needed to unburden
humanity of its neurosis. You might be surprised to know that during the First World War, psychologists became aware of a very
strange phenomenon. As long as the war continued, the proportion

of people who went mad fell almost to nil. Suicides were not committed, murders were not done, and people even stopped going mad. That was strange—what has that to do with war? Maybe murders are not done because murderers have gone into the army, but what happened to people who commit suicide? Maybe they have also joined the army, but then what happened to people who go mad? Have they even stopped going mad? Then again in the Second World War the same thing happened, in a greater proportion—and then the link was understood, the association. Humanity goes on accumulating a certain quantity of neurosis, madness. Each decade, it has to throw it out. So when there is war—war means when humanity has gone mad as a whole—then there is no need to go mad privately. What is the point? All are mad—then there is no point in trying to be privately mad. When one nation is murdering another, and there is so much suicide and murder, what is the point of doing these things on your own? You can simply watch the TV and enjoy, you can read it in the papers and have the thrill.

> People are not at ease within themselves, hence war has to exist, otherwise these people will go mad. Each decade a great war is needed to unburden humanity of its neurosis.

The problem is not war, the problem is individual neurosis.

Change the root—a radical transformation is needed; ordinary reformations won't do. But then you may not understand—I go on talking about meditation but you can't see the relationship, how meditation is related with war. I see the relationship; you don't see the relationship.

My understanding is this: that if even one percent of humanity becomes meditative, wars will disappear. And there is no other way.

> ❧
>
> If even one percent of humanity becomes meditative, wars will disappear. And there is no other way.

That much meditative energy has to be released. If one percent of humanity—that means one in a hundred people—becomes meditative, things will have a totally different arrangement. Greed will be less; naturally, poverty will be less. Poverty does not exist because things are scarce; poverty exists because people are hoarding, because people are greedy. If we live right now, there is enough; the earth has enough to give us. But we plan ahead, we hoard—then trouble arises.

Just think of birds hoarding . . . then a few birds will become rich and a few will become poor; then the American birds will become the richest and the whole world will suffer. But they don't hoard, so there is no poverty. Have you ever seen a bird poor? Animals in the forest—nobody is poor, nobody is rich. In fact, you don't even see fat birds and lean and thin birds. All the crows are almost alike; you cannot even recognize which is which. Why? They enjoy, they don't hoard.

Even to become fat means you are hoarding inside the body—that is a miserly mind. Misers become constipated; they cannot even throw out waste. They hoard; they control even defecation, they go on hoarding even rubbish. Hoarding is a habit with them.

To live in the moment, to live in the present, to live lovingly, to live in friendship, to care . . . then the world will be totally different. The individual has to change, because the world is nothing but a projected phenomenon of the individual soul.

Then he will be interested in the problems of the v.orld, but his interest will be of a different dimension. You may not even be able to understand it. People come to me and they say, "What are you doing? There is poverty and there is ugliness, and you go on teaching about meditation. Stop this. Do something about poverty." But nothing can be done about poverty directly. Meditative energy has to be released so people can enjoy the moment—then there will be no poverty. Communism is not going to destroy poverty; it has not destroyed it anywhere. It has created new sorts of poverty—and greater, and more dangerous. The communist is far poorer because he has lost his soul too. Now he is really not an individual at all—he has not even the freedom to pray and to meditate.

This is not going to help, this is destroying people. These are the do-gooders—avoid them.

And when a person meditates he starts flowering. If he is a painter, he will become a great painter. If he is a poet, then suddenly tremendous poetry will arise out of his soul. If he is a singer, for the first time he will sing a song that is close to his heart's desire.

When you are silent, rooted in your being, centered, your talents automatically start functioning. You start functioning the way existence always wanted you to function. You start functioning the way you were born to function, you start functioning the way your destiny wants you to function. You become spontaneous. You start doing your thing—and now you don't bother whether it pays or not, whether it makes you more respectable or not. It makes you happy, and that's enough. It makes you tremendously joyful, and that is more than enough.

But there are people who like to do things in a roundabout way. They would like to change the whole world first, and then they will come to themselves. But let me tell you, you will never be able to come to yourself if you go that far.

I have heard . . . An old man was sitting near Delhi and a young man was driving past. He came to a halt and asked the old man, "How far is Delhi?" The old man said, "If you go on the way you are going, and in the direction you are going, it is very, very far. You will have to travel the whole earth—because you have left Delhi two miles behind."

If you turn, then it is not very far—just a question of a few minutes. If you go on a journey to change the whole world and *then* you think you will change yourself, you will never be able to do it; you will never be able to come back home.

Start where you are. You are part of this ugly world and by changing yourself you are changing the world. What are you? A part of this ugly world. Why try to change your neighbor? He may not like it, he may not want it, he may not be interested. If you have become aware that the world needs a great change, then you are the closest world to yourself. Start from there.

Why am I always daydreaming about the future?

Everybody is doing that. The human mind as such is a daydreaming faculty. Unless you go beyond the mind, you will continue to daydream. The mind cannot exist in the present—it can either exist in the past or in the future. There is no way for the mind to exist in the present. To be in the present is to be without mind.

Try it. If there is a silent moment when no thought is crossing your being, your consciousness—when the screen of consciousness is absolutely unclouded—then suddenly you are in the present. That is the moment, the real moment—the moment of reality, the moment of truth. But then there is no past and no future.

Ordinarily, time is divided into these three tenses: past, present, future. The division is basically wrong, unscientific, because present is not part of time. Only past and future are parts of time. Present is beyond time. Present is eternity.

Past and future are part of time. The past is that which is no more, and the future is that which is not yet. Both are nonexistential. The present is that which is. The existential cannot be a part of the nonexistential. They never meet, they never cross each other's paths.

And time is mind; the accumulated past is what your mind is.

What is your mind? Analyze it, look into it. What is it? Just your past experiences piled up, accumulated. *Mind* is just a blanket term, an umbrella term; it simply holds your whole past, it is nothing else. If by and by you take your past out of the bag, the bag will disappear.

If the past is the only reality for the mind, then what can the mind do? One possibility is that it can go on

> The past is that which is no more, and the future is that which is not yet. Both are non-existential. The present is that which is.

chewing and rechewing the past again and again. That's what you call memory, remembrance, nostalgia. You go again and again backward; again and again to the past moments, beautiful moments, happy moments. They are few and far between, but you cling to them. You avoid the ugly moments, the miserable moments.

But this you cannot do all the time because this is futile; the activity seems to be meaningless. So the mind creates a "meaningful" activity—that's what daydreaming about the future is.

The mind says, "Yes, the past was good, but the past is finished; nothing can be done about it. Something can be done about the future because it is yet to come." So you choose out of your past experiences those which you would like to repeat again, and you drop the experiences that were very miserable, painful, and you don't want to repeat them in the future. Your future daydreaming is nothing but the past modified—better arranged, more decorated, more agreeable, less painful, more pleasant. This your mind goes on doing, and this way you go on missing reality.

Meditation simply means a few moments when you are not in the mind, a few moments when you slip out of the mind. You slip into reality, into that which is. These existential moments are so tremendously ecstatic that once you taste them, you will stop daydreaming.

Daydreaming will continue unless you start tasting meditation. Unless you are nourished on meditation, you will go on starving and hankering for some food in the future. And you know the future is not going to bring it, because today was the future just one day before. Yesterday, today was the future, and you were daydreaming about it. Now it is here. What is happening? Are you happy? Yesterday was also in the future at one time. The past was at one time all part of the future, and it has slipped by—and the future will also slip by. You are fooling yourself in your daydreaming.

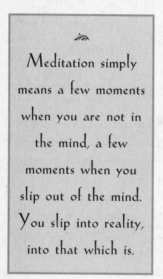

Meditation simply means a few moments when you are not in the mind, a few moments when you slip out of the mind. You slip into reality, into that which is.

Become a little more aware and try to bring your consciousness more and more to the facticity of existence. See *this* flower, don't think about *that* flower. Listen to *this* word I am uttering, not to *that* word I am going to utter. Look right now. If you postpone even for a single moment, you miss, and then it becomes a habit, a very ingrained habit. Tomorrow also you will miss, and the day after tomorrow also, because you will remain the same. Not only that—your habit of daydreaming will have become stronger.

The other night I was reading a Japanese story. Similar stories exist in all the folktales of the world. It is a beautiful story. Listen to it.

> There was once a man who hewed stones from the rock. His labor was very hard and he labored much, but his wages were slight and he was not content.

Who is content? Not even emperors are content, so what to say about a stonecutter? His work was certainly hard and the payoff was almost nothing.

> He sighed because his labor was hard, and he cried, "Oh, I wish I was rich so I could rest on a couch with a cover of silk." And an angel came from heaven, saying, "You are what you have said."

And this really happens—not only in parables and stories; it happens in real life. Whatever you think about yourself starts happening. You create your world by your thought, you create your world by your desire. Whatsoever you insist on starts happening. Reality goes on cooperating with you. It waits for the moment, for the day when *you* will cooperate with *it*. Until then, it goes on cooperating with you.

> And the angel said, "You are what you have said." And he was rich, and he rested on a couch, and the cover was of silk.
>
> The king of the land went by with horsemen in front of his carriage and behind the carriage there were also horsemen, and a golden parasol was held over the head of the king. When the rich man saw this, he was vexed that no golden parasol was held over his own head and he was not content. He sighed and cried, "I wish to be a king."

And the angel came again and he said, "You are what you have said."

Then he was king and many horsemen rode in front of his carriage, and there were also horsemen behind his carriage and a golden parasol was held over his head, and the sun shone hot rays and scorched the earth so that the grass shoots withered. And the king complained that the sun burned his face and that it excelled him in power and he was not content. He sighed and cried, "I wish to be the sun." And the angel came and he said, "You are what you have said." And he was the sun and he directed his rays upward and down, to the right and to the left, everywhere, and he scorched the grass shoots on earth, and the countenances of kings who were on earth.

Then a cloud placed itself between him and the earth, and the rays of the sun bounced back from it and he grew wrathful that his power was resisted. He complained that the cloud excelled him in power and he was not content. He wished to be the cloud, which was so powerful, and the angel came and he said, "You are what you have said."

And he became a cloud and placed himself between the sun and the earth and caught the rays so that the grass grew green. The cloud rained large drops on the earth, causing the rivers to swell and floods to carry the houses away, and he destroyed the fields with much water. He fell upon a rock that did not yield, and he splashed in great streams, but the rock did not yield, and he grew wrathful because the rock was not yielding to his power, and the power of his streams was in vain and he was not content.

He cried, "That rock has been given power which excels mine. I wish to be the rock." And the angel came and he was the rock, he did become the rock, and did not move when the sun shone or when it rained.

And then there was a man with a pick and with a chisel and with a heavy hammer, and he hewed stones out of the rock, and the rock said, "How can it be that this man has power that excels mine and hews stones out of my lap?" and he was not content.

He cried, "I am weaker than he. I wish to be that man." And the angel came from heaven, saying, "You are what you have said." He was a stonecutter again. And he hewed stones from the rock with hard labor, and he labored very hard for small wages—and he was content.

I don't agree with the conclusion. That is my only disagreement with the story; otherwise the story is beautiful. I don't agree with the conclusion because I know people—they cannot be so easily content. The wheel is complete, the story in a way has come to a natural end, but the real stories in life don't come to any natural end. The wheel again starts moving.

That's why in India we call life "the wheel." It goes on moving, goes on repeating itself. As far as I can see, unless the stonecutter became a buddha, the story would have been repeated again. Again he would become discontent. He would long for a beautiful couch and a cover of silk, and the same thing would start again. But if this stonecutter was really content, then he must have jumped out of the wheel of life and death. He must have become a buddha.

This is what goes on happening to each mind—you long for something, it will happen, but by the time it happens you will see that you are still discontent. Something else is creating the misery now.

This is something to be understood—if your desire is not fulfilled, you are frustrated; if it is fulfilled, then too you are frustrated. That is the misery of desire. Fulfilled, you are not fulfilled. Suddenly many new things arise.

You had never thought that when you are a king, and horsemen are in front of you and at the back of you, and a golden parasol is over your head, the sun can be so hot that it can scorch your face. You had never thought about it. Then you dreamed of becoming a sun, and you become a sun, and you had never thought about the cloud. Now the cloud is there and proving you impotent. And this goes on and on and on, like waves in the ocean, never-ending— unless you understand and simply jump out of the wheel.

The mind that goes on telling you, "Do this, be that. Possess this, possess that . . . otherwise how can you be happy if you don't have this? You have to have a palace, then you can be happy." If your happiness has a condition to it, you will remain unhappy. If you cannot be happy just as you are, just as a stonecutter . . . I know the labor is hard, wages are poor, life is a struggle, I know—but if you cannot be happy as you are, in spite of it all, you are not going to be happy ever. Unless a person is happy, simply happy for no reason at all, unless a person is mad enough to be happy without any reason, that person is not going to be happy ever. You will always find something destroying your happiness. You will always find something missing, something absent. And that "missing" will become your daydream again.

And you cannot achieve a state where everything, everything, is available. Even if it were possible, then too you would not be happy. Just look at the mechanism of the mind: If everything is available as you want it, suddenly you will feel bored. Now what to do?

I have heard this—and I think it is reliable—that people who have reached heaven are bored. It is from very reliable sources, you can depend on it—they are sitting under their wish-fulfilling trees and they are bored. Because the moment they say something, the angel appears and immediately he fulfills their desire. There is no gap between their desire and their fulfillment. They want a beautiful woman, a Cleopatra, and she is there. Now what to do with such a Cleopatra? It is pointless—and they get bored.

In Indian *Puranas* there are many stories of *devas* who became so bored in heaven that they started longing for the earth. They have everything there. When they were on the earth, they were hankering for heaven. They may have been great ascetics, they may have renounced the world, relationships, everything, to attain to heaven. Now they have reached heaven and they are hankering for the world.

I have heard:

The pilot of a new jet plane was winging over the Catskills and pointed out a pleasant valley to his second in command. "See that spot?" he demanded. "When I was a barefoot kid, I used to sit in a flat-bottomed rowboat down there, fishing. Every time a plane flew by, I would look up and dream I was piloting it. Now I look down and dream I am fishing."

That's how it goes, on and on. When you are not famous you want to be famous. You feel very hurt that people don't know you. You pass through the streets and nobody looks at you, nobody recognizes you. You feel like a nonentity. You do hard work to become famous. One day you become famous. Now you cannot move in the street. Now the crowd stares at you. You don't have any freedom, now you have to remain closed in your house. You cannot get out, you are imprisoned. Now you start thinking about those beautiful days when you used to walk on the streets and you were so free . . . as if you were alone. Now you hanker for those days. Ask the famous people.

Voltaire writes in his memoirs that when he was not famous—as everybody was one day not famous—he desired and desired and he worked hard, and he became one of the most famous men in France. His fame increased so much that it became almost dangerous for him to go out of his room, because in those superstitious days people used to think that if you can get a piece of the clothes of a very great man, it becomes a protection; it has tremendous protective value. It protects you against ghosts, against bad accidents and things like that.

So if he had to go out in public, he would go under police

escort, otherwise people would tear his clothes. Not only that—his skin would be torn, and he would come home bruised and bleeding. He became so fed up with this fame—he could not even get out of his house; people were always there like wolves to jump upon him—and he started praying to God, "Finished! I have known this. I don't want it. I have become almost a dead person." And then it happened. The angel came, must have come, and said, "Okay." By and by his fame disappeared.

People's opinions change very easily; they don't have any integrity. Just like fashion, things change. One day you are at the top of your fame, the next day people completely forget about you. One day you are the president; the next day you are just citizen Richard Nixon. Nobody bothers.

> Mind is a mechanism to create unhappiness. Its whole function is to create unhappiness. If you drop the mind, suddenly you become happy—for no reason at all.

It happened that people's minds changed, the opinion, the climate changed, and people completely forgot about Voltaire. He would go to the station and he would hope that at least someone, at least one person would be waiting there to receive him. Nobody would come to receive him, only his dog.

When he died, there were only four persons giving him a last good-bye; three were men and the fourth was his dog. He must have died in misery, again hankering for fame. What to do? This is how things go on.

The mind will never allow you to be happy. Whatever the condition, the mind will always find something to be unhappy about. Let me say it in this way: Mind is a mechanism to create unhappiness. Its whole function is to create unhappiness.

If you drop the mind, suddenly you become happy—for no reason at all. Then happiness is just natural, as you breathe. For breathing, you need not even be aware. You simply go on breathing. Conscious, unconscious, awake, asleep, you go on breathing. Happiness is exactly like that.

Happiness is your innermost nature. It needs no outside condition; it is simply there, it is you. Bliss is your natural state; it is not an achievement. If you simply get out of the mechanism of the mind, you start feeling blissful.

That's why you will see that mad people are happier than so-called sane people. What happens to mad people? They also get out of the mind—of course in a wrong way, but they get out of the mind. A madman is one who has fallen below the mind. He's out of the mind. That's why you can see that many mad people are so happy you can almost feel jealous. You can even daydream, "When will this blessing happen to me?" The madman is condemned, but he is happy.

What has happened to a madman? He is no longer thinking of the past and no longer thinking of the future. He has dropped out of time. He has started living in eternity.

It happens the same way to the mystic also, because he goes above mind. I am not telling you to become mad, but I am telling you that there is a similarity between the madman and the mystic. That's why all great mystics look a little mad and all great mad people look a little like mystics.

Watch a madman's eyes and you will find his eyes very mystical . . . a glow, some otherworldly glow, as if he has some inner door from where he reaches to the very core of life. He is relaxed. He may have nothing, but he is simply happy. He has no desires, no ambitions. He is not going anywhere. He is simply there . . . enjoying, delighting.

Yes, madmen and mystics have something similar. That similarity is because both are out of the mind. The madman has fallen below it, the mystic has gone beyond it. The mystic is also mad with a method; his madness has a method in it. The madman has simply fallen below.

I am not saying, Become mad. I am saying, Become mystics. The mystic is as happy as the mad and as sane as the sane. The mystic is as reasonable—even more reasonable—as so-called rational people, and yet so happy, just like mad people. The mystic has the most beautiful synthesis. He is in harmony. He has all that a reasonable man has. He has both. He is complete. He is whole.

You ask, "Why am I always daydreaming about the future?" You are daydreaming about the future because you have not tasted the present. Start tasting the present. Find a few moments where you are simply delighting. As you look at the trees, just be the look. As you listen to the birds, just be a listening ear. Let them reach to your deepest core. Let their song spread all over your being. As you sit by the side of the beach, just listen to the wild roar of the waves, become one with it . . . because that wild roar of the waves has no past, no future. If you can atune yourself to it, you will also become a wild roar. Hug a tree and relax into it. Feel its green shape rushing into your being. Lie down on the sand, forget the world, commune with the sand, the coolness of it; feel the coolness saturating you. Go to the river, swim, and let the river swim within you. Splash around and become the splashing. Do whatsoever you feel you enjoy, and enjoy it totally. In those few moments, the past and future will disappear and you will be here now.

The gospel is not in the Bible. The gospel is in the rivers and in the wild roar of the ocean and in the silence of the stars. The good news is written all over. The whole universe is a message. Decode it. Learn its language. Its language is that of here now.

Your language is that of past and future. So if you go on speaking the language of the mind, you will never be in tune, in harmony with existence. And if that harmony is not tasted, how can you stop daydreaming? Because that is what your life is.

It is as if a poor man is carrying a bag of ordinary stones, thinking that they are great diamonds, rubies, emeralds, and if you say to him, "Drop these. You are a fool. These are just ordinary stones," he cannot believe you. He will think you are tricking him. He will cling to them, because that's all he has.

I will not tell you that man to renounce his bag. I will try to show him real rubies, emeralds, diamonds. Just a glimpse of them and he will throw away the bag. Not that he will renounce it—because there is nothing to renounce; it is just full of ordinary stones. You don't renounce ordinary stones.

He will simply become aware that he was living under an illusion. Now there are real diamonds. Suddenly his own stones fade, they disappear. And he will simply empty his bag immediately without your telling him, because now he has something else to put in the bag. He will drop the stones because he needs the space.

So I don't say to you to drop going into the future, to drop going into the past. Rather, I would like to say to you, make more contacts with the present.

LIVE IN JOY

Live in joy, in love, even among those who hate.
Live in joy, in health, even among the afflicted.
Live in joy, in peace, even among the troubled.
Live in joy, without possessions, like the shining ones.
The winner sows hatred because the loser suffers.
Let go of winning and losing and find joy.

Meditate on these sutras of Gautama the Buddha. He is one of the most joyous persons ever. These sutras will give you immense insight into the heart of this awakened man:

Live in joy, in love, even among those who hate.

Joy is the key word of these verses. Joy is not happiness, because happiness is always mixed with unhappiness. It is never found in purity, it is always polluted. It always has a long shadow of misery behind it. Just as day is followed by night, happiness is followed by unhappiness.

Then what is joy? Joy is a state of transcendence. One is neither happy nor unhappy but utterly peaceful, quiet, in absolute equilibrium. So silent and so alive that one's silence is a song, that one's song is nothing but one's silence.

Joy is forever; happiness is momentary. Happiness is caused by the outside, hence can be taken away from the outside—you have to depend on others. And any dependence is ugly, any dependence is a bondage. Joy arises within, it has nothing to do with the outside. It is not caused by others; it is not caused at all. It is the spontaneous flow of your own energy.

If your energy is stagnant there is no joy. If your energy becomes a flow, a movement, a river, there is great joy—for no other reason, just because you become more fluid, more flowing, more alive. A song is born in your heart, a great ecstasy arises.

It is a surprise when it arises, because you cannot find any cause for it. It is the most mysterious experience in life: something uncaused, something beyond the law of cause and effect. It need not be caused because it is your intrinsic nature, you are born with it. It is something inborn, it is you in your totality, flowing.

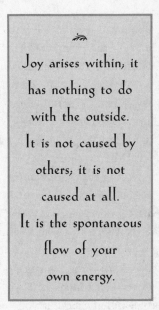

Joy arises within, it has nothing to do with the outside. It is not caused by others; it is not caused at all. It is the spontaneous flow of your own energy.

Whenever you are flowing, you are flowing toward the ocean. That is the joy: the dance of the river moving toward the ocean to meet the ultimate beloved. When your life is a stagnant pool you are simply dying. You are not moving anywhere—no ocean, no hope. But when you are flowing, the ocean is drawing closer every moment, and the closer the river comes the more dance there is, the more ecstasy there is.

Your consciousness is a river. Buddha has called it a continuum. It is a continuity, an eternal continuity, an eternal flow. Buddha has never thought about you and your being as something static. In his vision, the word *being* is not right. According to him, being is nothing but becoming. He denies being, he accepts becoming—because being gives you an idea of something static inside you, like a rock. Becoming gives you a totally different idea . . . like a river, like a lotus opening, like a sunrise. Something is constantly happening. You are not sitting there like a rock, you are growing.

Buddha changes the whole metaphysics: He replaces being with becoming, he replaces things by processes, he replaces nouns with verbs.

Live in joy . . . Live in your own innermost nature, with absolute acceptance of whosoever you are. Don't try to manipulate yourself according to others' ideas. Just be yourself, your authentic nature, and joy is bound to arise; it wells up within you. When the tree is taken care of, watered, looked after, it naturally blooms one day. When the spring comes there is great flowering. So is it with man. Take care of yourself. Find a right soil for your being, find a right climate, and go deeper and deeper into yourself.

Don't explore the world; explore your nature. Because by exploring the world you may have many possessions, but you will not be a master. However, by exploring yourself you may not have many possessions, but you will be a master. It is better to be a master of yourself than to be a master of the whole world.

Live in joy, in love . . . And one who lives in joy naturally lives in love. Love is the fragrance of the flower of joy. Inside there is joy; you cannot contain it. There is so much, it is unbearable. If you try to be miserly about it, you will feel pain. Joy can be so much that if you don't share it, it can become suffering, it can become pain.

Joy has to be shared; by sharing it you are unburdened, by sharing it you find new sources opening up within you, new streams, new springs. That sharing of your joy is love. Hence one thing has to be remembered: You cannot love unless you have attained to joy. And millions of people go on doing that. They want to love and they don't know anything about what joy is. Then their love is hollow, empty, meaningless. Then their love brings despair, misery, anguish; it creates hell. Unless you have joy you can't be in love. You have nothing to give, you are a beggar yourself. First you need to be a king—and your joy will make you a king.

When you are radiating joy, when your hidden secrets are no longer secrets but are flowering in the wind, in the rain, in the sun; when your imprisoned splendor is released, when your mystery has become an open phenomenon, when it is vibrating around you, pulsating around you—when it is in your breath, in your heartbeat—then you can love. Then you touch dust

> Joy has to be shared, by sharing it you are unburdened, by sharing it new sources open up within you, new streams, new springs. That sharing of your joy is love.

and the dust is transformed into the divine. Then whatever you touch becomes gold. Ordinary pebbles in your hand will be transmuted into diamonds, emeralds. Ordinary pebbles . . . people touched by you will not be ordinary anymore.

One who has attained joy becomes a source of great transformation for many people. His flame has been lit, now he can help others. The unlit flames, coming closer to the one who has become afire with joy, can also become lit. As you come closer, the flame jumps into you and you are never the same again.

Love is possible only when your flame is lit. Otherwise you are a dark continent—and you are pretending to give light to others? Love is light, hate is darkness. You are dark within and trying to give light to others? You will only succeed in giving them more darkness—and they are already in darkness. You will multiply their darkness, you will make them more miserable. Don't try to do that, because it is impossible, it is not according to the nature of things.

It can't happen. You can hope, but all your hope is in vain. First be filled with joy.

Live in joy, in love, even among those who hate. And then it is not a question of what others do to you. Then you can love even those who hate you. Then you can live in love and joy even amongst enemies. It is not just a question of loving those who love you. That is very ordinary, that is businesslike, a bargain. The real love is to love those who hate you. Right now, even to love those who love you is not possible, because you don't know what joy is. But when you know joy, the miracle happens, the magic. Then you are capable of loving those who hate you. In fact, it is no longer a question of loving somebody or not loving somebody, because you *become* love; you don't have anything else left.

In the Koran, I have heard, there is a statement, "Hate the devil." A great Sufi mystic woman, Rabiya, canceled that line from her Koran. Hassan, another famous mystic, was staying with Rabiya; he saw Rabiya doing it. He said, "What are you doing? The Koran cannot be corrected—that is blasphemy. You cannot cut any statement from the Koran; it is perfect as it is. There is no possibility of any improvement. What are you doing?"

Rabiya said, "Hassan, I have to do it! It is not a question of the Koran, it is something totally different: Since I have known God I cannot hate. It is not a question of the devil, I simply cannot hate. Even if the devil comes in front of me I will love him, because now I can only love; I am incapable of hate—that has disappeared. If one is full of light he can give you only light; whether you are a friend or an enemy does not matter.

"From where," Rabiya says, "can I bring darkness to throw on the devil? It is no longer anywhere—I am light. My light will fall on the devil as much as on God. Now, for me, there is no God and no devil, I cannot even make a distinction. My whole being is transformed into love; nothing is left.

"I am not correcting the Koran—who am I to correct it?—but

this statement is no longer relevant to me. And this is my copy; I am not correcting anybody else's Koran. I have the right to correct my copy according to myself. This statement hits me hard whenever I come across it. I cannot make any sense out of it; hence I am crossing it out."

One who is full of joy and love can't help it. One loves friends, one loves enemies. It is not a question of decision; love is now like breathing. Will you stop breathing if an enemy comes to see you? Will you say, "How can I breathe in front of my enemy?" Will you say, "How can I breathe because my enemy is also breathing and the air that has passed through his lungs may enter into mine? I can't breathe." You will suffocate, you will die. It will be suicide and utterly stupid.

On the way, a moment comes when love is just like breathing—the breathing of your soul. You go on loving.

In this light you can understand Jesus' statement: Love your enemies as yourself. If you ask Buddha, he will say: There is no need to do such a thing, because you can't do otherwise. You have to love. In fact you *are* love, so wherever you are—in flowers, in thorns, in the dark night, in the full noontide, in misery surrounding you like an ocean or in great success—it does not matter. You remain love; everything else becomes immaterial. Your love becomes something of the eternal, it continues. You may accept it, you may not accept it, but you can't hate; you have to be your true nature.

Live in joy, in health, even among the afflicted.

By *health* Buddha means wholeness. A healed person is a healthy person, a healed person is a whole person. By *health* Buddha does not mean the ordinary, medical definition of the term; his meaning is not medicinal, it is meditational—although you will be surprised to know that the words *meditation* and *medicine* both come from the same root. Medicine heals you physically, meditation heals you spiritually. Both are healing processes, both bring health.

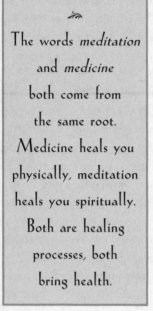

The words *meditation* and *medicine* both come from the same root. Medicine heals you physically, meditation heals you spiritually. Both are healing processes, both bring health.

But Buddha is not talking about the health of the body; he is talking about the health of your soul. Be whole, be total. Don't be fragmentary, don't be divided. Be an individual, literally—indivisible, one piece.

People are not one piece; they are many fragments, somehow holding themselves together. They can fall apart at any moment. They are all Humpty-Dumpties, just bundles of many things. Any new situation, any new danger, any insecurity, and they can fall apart. Your wife dies or you go bankrupt or you are unemployed—any small thing can prove to be the last straw. The difference is only of degree. Somebody is simmering at 98 degrees, somebody at 99; somebody may be at 99.9 degrees, but the difference is only of degree and any small thing can change the balance. You can go insane at any moment, because inside you are already a crowd. So many desires, so many dreams, so many people are living in you. If you watch carefully, you will not find one person inside but many faces, changing every moment. It is as if you are just a marketplace where so many people are going and coming, so much noise, and nothing makes sense. You go on accumulating.

Your childhood is the closest to buddhahood. As you grow old you grow insane. As you grow old, you go farther and farther away from buddhahood. It is really a very strange state; it should not be so. One should grow *toward* buddhahood, but people grow in just the opposite direction.

Buddha says:

Live in joy, in health, even among the afflicted.

This is a very important sutra to remember—more so because the Christians are creating a totally wrong approach to life. They say: When there is so much misery in the world, how can you be joyous? Sometimes they come to me and they say, "People are starving and people are poor. How can you teach people to dance and sing and be joyous? There are so many people afflicted with so many diseases, and you teach people meditation? This is selfishness!"

But that's exactly what Buddha is saying.

Live in joy, in peace, even among the troubled.

You cannot change the whole world. You have a small life span, it will be gone soon. You cannot make it a condition that "I will rejoice only when the whole world has changed and everybody is happy." That is never going to happen and it is not within your capacity to do it either. If the only way you can be happy is to have everybody else happy, then you are never going to be happy. Buddha is stating a simple fact. He is not saying, Don't help people, but rather, By being ill yourself you cannot help them.

By being poor yourself you cannot help the poor, although the poor will worship you because they will see how great a saint you are. They worshiped Mahatma Gandhi for the sheer reason that he tried to live like a poor man. But just by living like a poor man, you are not going to help the poor. If the doctor also falls ill to help his patients, will you call him a saint? You will just call him stupid, because this is the time he needs all his health, so that he can be helpful to people. This is strange logic, but it has prevailed down the centuries: that if you want to help the poor, be poor, live a poor life, live just like the poor. Of course the poor people will give you great respect and honor, but that is not going to help the poor, it will only fulfill your ego. And any ego fulfilled creates misery for you, not joy.

Live in joy, in health, even among the afflicted. Live in joy, in peace, even among the troubled. That is the only way to help, the only way to serve. First be selfish, first transform yourself. Your life in peace, in joy, in health, can be a great source of nourishment for people who are starving for spiritual food.

People are not really starving for material things. Material richness is very simple: just a little more technology, a little more science, and people can be rich. The real problem is how to be inwardly rich. And when you are outwardly rich you will be surprised—for the first time you become more acutely, more keenly, aware of your inner poverty. For the first time all meaning in life disappears when you are outwardly rich, because in contrast, your inner poverty can be seen more clearly. Outside there is light all around and inside you are a dark island.

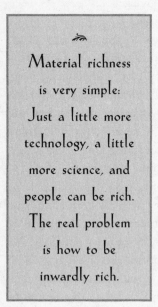

Material richness is very simple: Just a little more technology, a little more science, and people can be rich. The real problem is how to be inwardly rich.

The rich man feels his poverty more than the poor person, because the poor person has no contrast. Outside there is darkness, inside there is darkness; he knows darkness is what life is. But when there is light outside, you become desirous of a new phenomenon: You long for inner light. When you see that richness is possible outside, why can't you be rich inside?

Live in joy, without possessions, like the shining ones.

Enjoy the world, enjoy the sun, the moon, the stars, the flowers, the sky, the earth. Live in joy and peace, without possessiveness. Don't possess. Use, but don't possess—because the possessor cannot use. The possessor really becomes possessed by his own possessions. That's why so many rich people become so miserable; they live a poor life. They have all the money in the world, but they live in a poor way.

The richest man in the world, just a few decades ago, was the Nizam of Hyderabad—the richest man in the world. In fact, his riches were so great that nobody has ever been able to estimate how much he had. His treasuries were full of diamonds; everything was made of diamonds. Even his paperweight was the biggest diamond in the world; the Kohinoor is only one third the size of his paperweight.

When he died, his paperweight was found in his shoe. The diamonds were not counted because there were so many. They were weighed, not counted—how many kilos, not how many diamonds—who could count? Each year the diamonds were brought out of the basements. He had the biggest palace in India, but all the roofs were not enough, because his diamonds were spread on the roofs of his palace just to give them a little sunlight every year. But the man lived a life of such misery, you cannot believe it; even beggars live far better.

He used to collect cigarettes that others had already smoked and thrown away—just cigarette butts. He would not purchase cigarettes for himself, he would collect these cigarettes and smoke them. Such a miser! For fifty years he used only a single cap—it was so dirty and stinking! He died in the same cap. He never used to change his clothes. And it is said that he used to purchase his clothes from the secondhand marketplace where old, rotten things, used things, are sold. His shoes must have been the dirtiest in the world, but he would only send them once in a while for repair, he would not purchase new shoes.

Now, the richest man in the world living in such misery and miserliness—what had happened to this man? Possessiveness! Possessiveness was his disease, his mania. He wanted to possess everything. He would purchase diamonds all over the world; wherever there were diamonds his agent was there to purchase them. Just have more and more! But you cannot eat diamonds—and he was eating the poorest kind of food. He was so afraid that he was unable to sleep at all—in constant fear that somebody might steal from him.

That's how the paperweight—the costliest diamond that he had, three times greater in weight than the Kohinoor—was found in his shoe. When he was dying he had hidden it in his shoe so nobody could steal it—otherwise the paperweight would be too visible, too much in front of the eyes of people. Even dying he was more concerned with the diamond than with his own life. He could never give anything to anybody.

This happens to people who become possessive: They don't use things, they are used by things. They are not masters, they are servants of their own things. They go on accumulating and they die without ever having enjoyed all that they had.

Live in joy, without possessions, like the shining ones.

Live like the buddhas, who don't possess a thing but can use everything. The world has to be used, not possessed. We come empty-handed and we go empty-handed, so there is no point in possessing anything. To be possessive is ugly. But use everything! While you are alive, use the world; enjoy everything the world makes available and then go without looking back, without clinging to things.

> The world has to be used, not possessed. We come empty-handed and we go empty-handed, so there is no point in possessing anything.

The intelligent person uses life and uses it beautifully, aesthetically, sensitively. Then the world has many treasures for him. He never becomes attached, because the moment you become attached you have fallen asleep.

The winner sows hatred because the loser suffers.

Let go of winning and losing and find joy.

How to find joy? Let your ambition disappear; ambition is the barrier. Ambition means an ego trip: "I want to be this, I want to be that—more money, more power, more prestige." But remember, *The winner sows hatred because the loser suffers. Let go of winning and losing and find joy.* If you want to find joy, forget about winning and losing. Life is a play, a game. Play it beautifully, forget all about losing and winning.

The real sportsman's spirit is not that of winning or losing, that is not his real concern. He enjoys playing. That is the real player. If you are playing to win, you will play with tension, anxiety. You are not concerned with the play itself, its joy and its mystery; you are more concerned with the outcome. This is not the right way to live in the world.

Live in the world without any idea of what is going to happen. Whether you are going to be a winner or a loser, it doesn't matter. Death takes everything away. Whether you lose or win is immaterial. The only thing that matters, and it has always been so, is how you played the game. Did you enjoy it?—the game itself? Then each moment is a moment of joy.

About the Author

O sho's teachings defy categorization, covering everything from the individual quest for meaning to the most urgent social and political issues facing society today. His books are not written but are transcribed from audio and video recordings of extemporaneous talks given to international audiences over a period of thirty-five years. Osho has been described by the *Sunday Times* in London as one of the "1,000 Makers of the 20th Century" and by American author Tom Robbins as "the most dangerous man since Jesus Christ."

About his own work Osho has said that he is helping to create the conditions for the birth of a new kind of human being. He has often characterized this new human being as "Zorba the Buddha"— capable of enjoying both the earthy pleasures of a Zorba the Greek and the silent serenity of a Gautam Buddha. Running like a thread through all aspects of Osho's work is a vision that encompasses both the timeless wisdom of the East and the highest potential of Western science and technology.

Osho is also known for his revolutionary contribution to the science of inner transformation, with an approach to meditation that acknowledges the accelerated pace of contemporary life. His unique "Active Meditations" are designed to first release the accumulated stresses of body and mind, so that it is easier to experience the thought-free and relaxed state of meditation.

Osho® Meditation Resort

⌒⌒⌒

The Osho Meditation Resort is a place where people can have a direct personal experience of a new way of living with more alertness, relaxation, and fun. Located about one hundred miles southeast of Mumbai in Pune, India, the resort offers a variety of programs to thousands of people who visit each year from more than a hundred countries around the world.

Originally developed as a summer retreat for maharajas and wealthy British colonialists, Pune is now a thriving modern city that is home to a number of universities and high-tech industries. The meditation resort spreads over forty acres in a tree-lined suburb known as Koregaon Park. The resort campus provides accommodation for a limited number of guests, and there is a plentiful variety of nearby hotels and private apartments available for stays of a few days up to several months.

Resort programs are all based on the Osho vision of a qualitatively new kind of human being who is able both to participate creatively in everyday life and to relax into silence and meditation. Most programs take place in modern, air-conditioned facilities and include a variety of individual sessions, courses, and workshops covering everything from creative arts to holistic health treatments, personal transformation and therapy, esoteric sciences, the "Zen" approach to sports and recreation, relationship issues, and significant life transitions for men and women. Individual sessions and group workshops are offered throughout the year, alongside a full daily schedule of meditations.

Outdoor cafes and restaurants within the resort grounds serve both traditional Indian fare and a choice of international dishes, all made with organically grown vegetables from the commune's own farm. The campus has its own private supply of safe, filtered water.

For more information about Osho and his work, see:

www.osho.com

This is a comprehensive Web site in several languages, featuring an online tour of the meditation resort, a calendar of its course offerings, a catalog of books and tapes, a list of Osho information centers worldwide, and selections from Osho's talks.

Or contact:

Osho International
New York
e-mail: oshointernational@oshointernational.com

OSHO®

LOOK WITHIN...

TAO: THE PATHLESS PATH

Contemporary interpretations of selected parables from the *Lieh Tzu* reveal how the timeless wisdom of this 2500-year-old Taoist classic contains priceless insights for living today.

ISBN: 1-58063-225-4 Paperback $11.95/$17.95 Can.

YOGA: THE SCIENCE OF THE SOUL

Modern yoga emphasizes physical postures and exercises to increase flexibility and aid in relaxation. But yoga has its roots in the understanding of human consciousness and its potential. Explore this potential with Osho's unique insights into yoga and its relationship to the modern mind.

ISBN: 0-312-30614-8 Paperback $12.95/$18.95 Can.

ZEN: THE PATH OF PARADOX

"Zen is not a philosophy, it is poetry. It does not propose, it simply persuades. It does not argue, it simply sings its own song. It is aesthetic to the very core." In this book, Osho calls Zen "the path of paradox" and unfolds the paradox through delightful Zen anecdotes and riddles.

ISBN: 0-312-32049-3 Paperback $11.95/$17.95 Can.

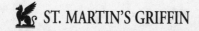